# Why Don't You Convert?

## and Other Short Stories

K L Chowdhury

Vitasta

*Let Knowledge Spread*

Published by
Renu Kaul Verma
Vitasta Publishing Pvt Ltd
2/15, Ansari Road, Daryaganj
New Delhi - 110 002
info@vitastapublishing.com

ISBN 978-93-82711-64-3


All the names and the characters in this book are fictitious. Resemblance to anyone, living or dead, is purely coincidental.



Typeset and Cover Design by Vits Press

# Contents

# Dedication

To my patients, the heroes and heroines of my stories.

You have regarded me variously as a healer, mentor and saviour, but I look upon you as my guru at whose bedside I endeavour to perfect the art of healing. I thank you for the trust you placed in me.

# Preface

The practice of medicine is a marriage of science and art. It is an exciting and challenging experience, at once elevating and humbling, mystifying and ennobling. It is knowledge applied in real time on real people – the complex and dynamic organism that is the human being. The patient, being the central character, who willingly or by force of circumstance becomes the subject, also turns out to be the quintessential teacher. The art demands of the practitioner more than mere knowledge and experience. It demands a strong self-belief, a lot of passion, and a large measure of insight and empathy. What is commonly called the healing touch may remain a chimera without these attributes. For all the rapid and breathtaking technological advances, and the slow but certain invasion of the medical profession by the robot and the computer that has the inherent danger of turning this art into mere craft, nothing can replace the human touch. That touch embodies the connectivity between human beings, in this case between a doctor and his patient, and the trust that the latter places on his experience and judgment.

# Acknowledgement

I don't have enough words to thank my teachers, colleagues and students, whom I came across during my long career, for having shared their ideas and experiences with me to make this journey exciting, adventurous and rewarding.

I am immensely grateful to Bodhji (Surinder) for his painstaking and meticulous editing of most of the stories in this collection, to Baiji (Robin) for his imaginative and insightful suggestions, to Leku (Anita) for the final flourishes and to Leela for her patience and perseverance while I remained glued to the laptop.

My special thanks to the irrepressible Veena Batra, the vastly talented editor at Vitasta, who infects you with her energy and dynamism. She used her discretion in choosing from the thirty-five stories that I had submitted, and in giving them the final order in which they have appeared in print.

Renu Kaul Verma, the publisher of Vitasta, deserves my special gratitude for her faith in me, for her cooperation, for her dogged persistence in getting some of the stories out of me that I had reserved for a future publication. She did my first collection of short stories '*Faith and Frenzy*' and I am hoping there will be more engagements in the coming days.

If it were not for my friend, M K Raina, who nudged me to write for *Harvan*, these stories might have remained in my memory bank, never to see the light of print. I am highly grateful to him.

# Author's Note

Several years ago a pharmaceutical representative finished detailing me his products and, then, rather abruptly, asked me: "Sir, what is your philosophy at work?" I was somewhat surprised by this sudden change of subject. Without giving it much conscious thought I replied, almost equally brusquely, "*Listen to the patient.*" He seemed a bit baffled with my short answer and sat there waiting for more. Realising that I had said all that I intended to, he thanked me and left.

A couple of months later, he returned and presented me a plaque. It bore my name with an inscription, *My philosophy at work: Listen to the patient.* I had all but forgotten about this! However, since that day the plaque rests on my desk as an emblem of my work ethic.

As someone who loves to *listen* to stories, I am fortunate to be a practicing doctor who comes across a wide spectrum of humanity. Every patient has a story to tell. Apart from the fact that more than ninety per cent of the diagnoses come from listening to the patients, the stories themselves are often interesting and engaging—they are, after all, *human* stories, each unique in its own way.

I also love to narrate stories. I generally jot down notes of interesting patients in my diary, but many of the fascinating stories that I glean from my patients also remain stored away in the closets of my memory. It does not take much effort to pull them out almost as fresh as when they were received.

Some time back, my friend, M K Raina, invited me to write a regular health column for *Harvan*, the e-magazine he was editing. After thinking over his proposal, I decided to approach the subject unconventionally and not in the familiar textbook format — an exercise that often proves to be impersonal and boring, and burdens the readers with a lot of facts, controversial at times, that they could do without. Instead, I chose to offer a selection of case vignettes from my long experience as a practicing physician and, in the process, recount some of the most compelling cases—diagnostic dilemmas, unsolved problems, missed diagnosis, tragic outcomes, and triumphs (which the patients gratefully call miracles).

I accepted the brief and started writing the stories. These

stories trace my medical journey spanning over five decades, and give the reader a fair idea of the times, the places and the people that I came across in my practice. They unfold the demands and challenges, the excitements and adventures, the agony of failures and the ecstasy of triumphs in the life of a doctor while dealing with his patients, whose lives get intricately interwoven with his own. They speak of the doctor's crusade not only against disease, but also against ignorance and entrenched belief, of the frailty of the patient on the one hand and his steely survival instinct on the other, of the natural course of a disease as against an unexpected and unexplained turn of events that remind the practitioner of the large grey areas in the knowledge and practice of medicine.

*Harvan* stopped publishing after a brief stint, but I did not stop writing, for there is no end to human stories. I am now taking the opportunity of presenting these and other stories in this compilation.

All the stories presented here are drawn from true events, even though many of them sound stranger than fiction. I believe there is a thin line separating the two. These are stories about people who seek comfort and cure at the hands of the doctor, a mortal like anyone else, but often deified and looked upon as a messiah. They are not just bare descriptions of diseases, but an empathy-filled portrait of the patients and their close kin and caregivers. Above all, they provide a flavour of medical practice in India, and how it has evolved from the seventies of the last century — when the clinical skills of the doctor and not the diagnostic tools were pre-eminent in treating disease — to the present times.

I believe my stories should interest the common reader who is scared of falling ill, awed by the doctors, wary of the investigations, and enthralled by the aura of mystery and inscrutability about illness, about life and death. The readers will not only get a closer peep into the lives of patients but also find in some of the stories an echo of their own experiences, as also an insight into the eventful lives of the doctors into whose hands they entrust the most precious thing they posses — their *own* lives.

I also believe that the stories should equally interest the medical professionals who, during their busy lives, often tend to forget how they have been specially placed by destiny to play a pivotal role as a caregiver, friend, confidante and healer; who, like detectives, hurl themselves into the cases, going back and forth in the sequence of events, looking for signs, digging for clues, watching the developments, marshalling the investigative tools and interventions as the situation demands, in an attempt to nail the culprit—the affliction from which their patient is suffering.

K L Chowdhury
February 2015
Jammu

# Why Don't You Convert?

Meera Bhat consulted me for poor appetite, disturbed sleep, suffocation, and bouts of palpitation that had started soon after she took up a teaching assignment in Kashmir. Anxiety was writ large on her face and in her demeanour. Notwithstanding, she proved to be a good narrator and readily answered my questions.

Meera was twenty-five-years-old. She was six when her parents fled their Habba Kadal home in Kashmir. Islamic militants had given them a twenty-four hour notice to leave or face death. On a freezing January morning, her father hurriedly dumped the few clothes he could get hold of into a suitcase and hoisted Meera on his shoulders. His wife grabbed son Ashutosh's arm and the family walked out of their home to catch the first taxi passing by that would take them out of the valley. By evening they landed in a *serai* on the outskirts of Jammu where they set up home for three months, moving into a rented room for three years and, finally, graduating to the Mishriwalla Migrant Camp built by the government for thousands of Kashmiri refugees like them.

Eighteen years after the 1990 mass exodus of the Kashmiri Pandits, Prime Minister Manmohan Singh announced a package for their rehabilitation. Among other sops, the half-baked package included 6000 jobs for their youth, to be funded and financed by the Central Government. By that time Meera had completed her masters in English and, with much difficulty, got a job in a private school at a meagre salary with which she could barely support herself, let alone her family.

It took the exiled community three years, numerous appeals and memoranda, and umpteen meetings with mandarins and ministers before the State Government of J&K bothered to open the prime minister's package and create 1500 jobs for their unemployed youth. Several stringent preconditions, all contrary to the existing rules and regulations for state employees, were attached to the jobs—that the recruits would be posted only in their home districts from where they had been hounded out two decades earlier, that they would not seek transfer anywhere else, that they would not leave the station without prior permission, and that they would not be entitled to any superannuation on retirement. They were to make their own arrangements for lodgings until such time as the administration built living quarters for them. There were no provisions for their safety and security. In short, they would work there, live there, and die there.

After much debate in the family, Meera gave up her job at Jammu in favour of the government job at Srinagar which paid nearly thrice what she was earning. She had been selected as a teacher in a Government High School at Budgam. She had hazy memories of her childhood in Kashmir but the images she had formed of the place from various accounts as she grew up in exile were forbidding. It was with mixed feelings that she boarded the bus to Srinagar along with her father. They took a room on rent near her school and he stayed with her until she completed the tortuous official formalities.

When he left, Meera's father had parting words for her: "Daughter, it is an odd twist of fate that we had to rent a room for you when you should have moved into our own home at Habba Kadal where you were born. The house was vandalised after we were forced to flee; I hear it is now in total ruin. It will break our hearts to go there anytime soon. We might consider visiting the place someday after you settle down. Meanwhile, I would like you to remember that you are now an ambassador of your community in your own homeland. So are all the other new recruits. It should be your endeavour to focus on your job and give your best to the students. You should avoid engaging in debates or discussions on politics, religion, militancy and related topics, and try to be friendly with everyone. That might help generate a feeling of goodwill so vital for re-establishing the old fraternal ties between the two estranged communities."

"Father, you are asking the victims to placate the criminals?" Meera could not resist asking.

"My dear, it is time to revive the spirit of Kashmiriyat if we want to return to our homeland. The onus has always been on us to keep it alive. I realise it is not going to be easy for you to live in the changed milieu of Kashmir, not easy with the conditions akin to bonded labour that are attached to your job. But you have to give it your best shot."

ꟸꟸ

Meera—pink, pretty, and slim — created a stir in the school in the very first week with her attractive demeanour, outgoing ways, and penchant for teaching. She was assigned the students of eleventh and twelfth grades. She hardly ever missed a class, insisted on punctuality, and taught with passion. She enforced discipline, encouraged questions, and assigned homework to the students that demanded their wholehearted participation. For them, she was like a breath of fresh air.

But life was not easy for the new recruits in Kashmir. Meera was allotted a room in the residential complex at Sheikhpura, a few kilometres away from her school, which she had to share with another recruit. There was barely enough space to stretch her limbs, let alone inviting any of her own visiting kin even for a single night. Besides a Sikh female colleague, Meera was the only Pandit amongst the staff of fifteen. There were no Pandit students in the school. The whole ambience in the school was Islamic. The day started with a Muslim prayer; the dress code, the academic calendar and the school functions were Islamic in content and character. Sometimes she wondered if she was on an alien planet where the customs and rituals, mannerisms and conversational nuances, greetings and colloquialisms, jokes and invocations were all different from hers. There was nothing common with these people except that she looked like them and spoke Kashmiri, albeit with an accent. During the early days, when she went about with her head bare, she met with raised eyebrows. So she decided to wear a scarf to cover her head. Gradually, in an attempt to communicate with her students and colleagues in their idiom, she unknowingly acquired some of their mannerisms and lingo. Even as she found her colleagues generally friendly and polite, there seemed an unbridgeable gulf between them because of their brazenly anti-Indian rhetoric and an untiring preoccupation with religion. She seemed to live a false and constricted existence that suffocated her inside. There was nowhere to go after school hours, no family, no social life. She suffered a deep sense of loss and missed the free and fraternal spirit that she had grown up with living in the refugee camp at Jammu. She missed her friends, missed going to the temple with her mother, missed the festivals and other social functions. She turned vegetarian for she could never be sure if it was beef or lamb that was being sold in the shops.

Her salary was not released for three months on one pretext or another until she found out that she had to grease the palms of every functionary in the official hierarchy — the peons who passed the files from one table to another, the clerks who managed the files, the treasury officials who passed the bills, the cashier who delivered the pay cheques and so on.

With every passing day, the strain proved too much and symptoms of anxiety started weighing her down. She found herself crying silently in bed after a day's work. That is when she came to pay her first visit to her parents, and her father accompanied her to my clinic.

The interview passed off well and proved a cathartic one for her. I advised her to eschew the negative reactions. After all, these were early days; it would take some time to settle down and find her space. Besides, she was not alone in this; there were another fifteen hundred recruits like her going through the same travails. She had to prove to herself and her family that she was no coward.

I prescribed anti-anxiety pills and asked her to see me again on her next visit to her parents.

ꕥ

Armed with renewed determination, Meera returned to Kashmir, cheered up after spending three days with her family in the Jagti Township built for the exiled people where they had moved. She assumed a breezy stance and resumed teaching with fervour. She became popular with everyone and was a darling of the students, some of whom in the adolescent and pubescent age groups were quite enamoured of her. Since she was a friendly and frank mentor, they spoke freely with her, sometimes asking very personal questions. She did not mind some degree of their inquisitiveness.

One day, while checking the essay, *The Essence of Religions*, that her students had chosen to write, Aslam, a twelfth grade student asked her, "Madam, do you believe in Islam?"

The abrupt question surprised her and it took her a while to answer.

"I believe in all religions that teach brotherhood and peace."

"That is what Islam stands for, Madam."

"I hope its votaries make that a guiding theme of their lives."

"And Islam teaches compassion," he went on.

"Compassion is an even greater virtue."

"But you are not Muslim?"

"No, I am not; nor am I without compassion."

He was a bit nonplussed. "What is your religion, Madam?"

"I am a Hindu."

"Islam is a great religion."

"All religions lead to the same God."

"But Islam is the best."

"It is the believers who make religion good or bad."

"Madam, why don't you accept Islam?" he said ingratiatingly.

"I have not rejected it."

"I mean, why don't you convert?"

"Convert?"

"Yes, convert to Islam."

"My conversion won't make Islam any better. Besides, I have no problem with being what I am."

The boy shrugged his shoulders in a gesture of helplessness, excused himself and left. But Meera was left with more questions than her student had posed. Why should a twelfth grader try to motivate her to change her religion?

She did not have to wait long for the answer.

Majid, another twelfth grader asked her on another day, "Madam, when are you going to marry?"

"I am in no hurry. Why do you ask?"

"We are all keen to know who will be the lucky man."

"I haven't given it much thought yet."

"But you are already settled in a job. You are alone. You need a husband," he spoke with bravado, his eyes smiling.

"I don't need a husband but a husband may need me." She winked at him playfully.

"That is one and the same thing," he replied, feeling emboldened.

"It is not. Go home and think about it," she said dismissively.

Majid was not to be put off by her ready wit. "But there might be someone who does need you."

"In that case, and when it is time, I will consider."

"What about Mushtaq sir?"

She gave him a severe look, flabbergasted at his audacity. Was this boy in his senses to suggest a husband for her!

But Majid was unfazed. "Madam, I am speaking of the Urdu teacher. Isn't he a good choice – noble and handsome? He is from a decent family; they have orchards, mills and other businesses."

"That doesn't interest me. Besides, I am a Hindu as you

might know."

"What is wrong in marrying a Muslim? Is Islam not the best of all religions?"

Here was another boy speaking the same language.

"All the same I am quite happy being a Hindu. I love my religion like you seem to love yours."

"What is your religion all about except worshipping stones and pictures of funny gods, some with several arms and others with elephant heads, riding rats?"

She gave a hearty laugh. "Well, I don't expect you to you to understand the deep symbolism in our fantastic legends, and the riveting stories in our epics."

"I have watched the Mahabharata. In Hinduism it seems there is adultery all over the place; your gods seduce women and they bear illegitimate children who go to war with each other."

Meera did not lose her self assurance. "This is preposterous. I don't like my students to be so deluded. If you really want to know about other religions, you should try to explore and understand, and not denigrate them. It goes against ethics, against your Islam. Besides, you confuse religion with the epics."

"Then what is your religion if not the Mahabharata and Ramayana?"

"It is a lot more. It is the Vedas and Upanishads; it is the great philosophy enshrined in the Gita; it is the higher truths of life that the sages sought answers for."

"Madam, if you don't mind, could you tell me why you worship stones?"

He was going too far, and she decided to cut him short. "So do you when you go on the pilgrimage to Mecca. There, you walk in a circle around the Kaaba that holds a black stone inside – a stone every Muslim considers sacred and holy."

Cut to the quick, Majid beat a hasty retreat without *salaaming* her as was the custom when students took leave of their teachers.

But many more disturbing questions arose in Meera's head. Was it just the inquisitiveness and impetuosity of juveniles or was she the victim of a subtle conspiracy? Why was religion the most dominant theme in Kashmir, occupying almost all the social and mental space? Why were even small children and teenagers preoccupied with it when they should be engaged with studies and games?

There were other thoughts too troubling Meera – on the home front. Her parents were eager to see her settled in matrimony. They had resumed visits to the matchmakers after she got the teaching job, and there were a couple of proposals. Shivratri was near and she was visiting home for a four-day sojourn to celebrate the festival with her family. Her parents had arranged for her to meet two prospective grooms during this time.

The first interview was a failure from the start. The candidate was a deputy manager with a manufacturing firm at Gangyal. He was loudmouthed and boorish, cynical and full of himself. He boasted unabashedly about his status in the factory, the trust that his boss placed in him and the fear that he instilled in the workers. He felt no compunction asking her what portion of her salary she set aside for her parents who, he had the cheek to remind her, had no source of income other than the government dole, and, how much she lavished on her unemployed older brother. It incensed her and she dropped him like a hot potato.

The second interview started off well with the usual introductions and preliminary questioning. He was an arts graduate, running an electronic goods shop that earned him a reasonable income. He lived with his parents who had built a small house at Muthi soon after the exodus from Kashmir. She liked his forthrightness and she seemed to suit all his requirements for a wife except that she was posted in Kashmir.

"I don't know how to say this, but if we agree to marry, you may have to leave your job," he said.

"I worked hard to get this job. It will be a terrible disappointment to give it up," she replied.

"We can't to get married and live in two different cities 300 km apart, with not many opportunities of meeting and living together, given your service rules and working conditions," he said.

"We have to face the fact that Pandit boys and girls are barred from government jobs in Jammu, and the chances of getting an equivalent job in the private sector are remote. Rather than I giving up my job it may be more practical for you to set up your business in Kashmir," she suggested.

"It has taken me several years and a lot of hard work to establish my business in Jammu. It will take me much longer to find a shop, a house, and to set up a business in Kashmir. Until then, I don't want to become a laughing stock for living off my wife's earnings. By now you should know better than me what it takes to start life all over again in Kashmir for people who were driven out from there. To be frank, I hate the very idea of living in a place where we are not welcome."

She could not fault his argument, nor was she prepared to give up her hard-earned job.

Even as she put up a bold face, the failure to make any headway on the matrimonial front did not leave her unscathed. Her anxiety resurfaced and she came to consult me a second time before her return to Kashmir.

An element of depression had crept into the clinical picture besides the resurgent anxiety. She sighed often during the interview, broke down a couple of times, and expressed her disenchantment with marriage. It took a long session of counselling to calm her down. She was a self-made woman, I explained to her; she didn't need anyone's advice to guide her life, and certainly not the crutch of a man to survive. My pep talk revived her self-confidence quite a bit and I saw her smile for the first time at the end of the interview.

Meera returned to her job in Kashmir and settled into a rhythm where life goes on from one day to another without much happening and with little expectation of change — an uneasy calm which descends from being trapped in drabness and monotony that tend to become a habit over time. She went about her job, trying to recapture her passion for teaching, bonding with students, fraternising with colleagues. For some time she all but forgot about matrimony.

Then a strange wind blew. Her father informed her about a fresh marriage proposal. She replied that she was not interested in going through the ordeal of another interview but he prevailed upon her not to let go of this opportunity. As with the earlier proposals, the *teknis* had been matched and a propitious day was fixed for a meeting with the prospective groom. He had agreed to travel to Srinagar since Meera was denied permission to leave the station.

On a bright Sunday morning in July, Meera Bhat met Rajesh Razdan in the premises of the Hanuman Temple.

They sat on the steps of the river *ghat*. The Amiarkadal Bridge, in full view from there, was already alive with traffic; the Vitasta flowed quietly underneath it and beyond on her undulating course. A cool breeze blew gently into their faces as the interview progressed over home-made *aaloo parathas* that Meera's mother had asked her to carry along.

Rajesh was an engineering graduate, looking for a job and a wife. Fair and good looking, he seemed the prototype of a self-opinionated Kashmiri Pandit, brandishing his scholastic accomplishments and his family antecedents, waxing eloquent on his views on cultural traditions and family ties. He evinced keen interest in her educational qualifications, even her marks and percentages in different examinations; her likes and dislikes; her culinary skills; her parents and brother; her friends, cousins and others. He asked her about her salary and her savings. It went on for about an hour. Meera tried to answer all his queries without losing her calm. That is what her mother had begged of her. But she felt an irritation rising within her when he asked what gifts she would bring for his parents, siblings, uncles and aunts. She firmly replied that she had no idea what her parents had kept aside for the dowry and gifts, but it would be within their means.

"I am quite happy with the interview, Miss Bhat," he said finally, like an examiner declaring the result of a student, arrogance oozing from his speech and demeanour.

"Thank you," she said half-heartedly.

"But there is a snag."

She looked at him with an expression, half surprise, half sarcasm, waiting for him to continue.

"Your mother is not a Kashmiri."

This crude statement was like the proverbial last straw that broke her reserve, and she asked the first question during the whole interview. "May I please know how she is not a Kashmiri?"

A bit put off by her curt response, he said, "I hear she is from Doda?"

"You sound as if she is from an alien planet. I hope you know that Doda is a part of the state of Jammu and Kashmir. In any case, is that a disqualification?"

"But she is not a Kashmiri Pandit, not a *Batni*."

"My mother is as staunch a *Batn*i as there ever was, and certainly better than others who parade their lineage," she snapped. "Look at this river. It is Vitasta where it takes birth from the spring at Verinag. It remains Vitasta all through its long course, and it still is Vitasta when it finally merges into the sea. My mother was a Kashmiri Pandit when her parents were hounded out from the valley centuries back like we have been thrown out now in 1990. Exile does not change your origins or name."

Rajesh was amazed at her repartee and fumbled for words. Then he made another faux pas: "You see, our families don't match."

"What is the mismatch about?" she demanded.

"We belong to the famous Razdan clan from Safakadal," he continued.

When she heard the word clan, her eyes flashed in anger. Looking him in the face, she snapped, "Was it not one of your clan who would go home drunk and beat up his wife and kids?"

Grievously outsmarted, he looked at her in disbelief, and just managed to stammer, "I am not aware of any such person. In any case, what has that to do with our marriage?"

"The same as my mother being from Doda; the same as the demands you make for dowry and gifts for your uncles and aunts. Look here, I am proud to be the daughter of a woman from Doda. Your family could learn a lesson or two in cultural traditions and graces from her. I don't understand why, if you had a problem with my mother's origins, did you come for this meeting?"

He found himself in a predicament. She certainly presented herself as an accomplished and intelligent girl, but he had spoilt the interview.

He tried to make amends. "I am sorry; I didn't mean to say anything bad about your mother. And you misunderstood me about the gifts. Giving gifts to elders is just a gesture of respect. I was merely curious, not seeking dowry."

"I don't know why no one ever thought of giving gifts to

the parents of the bride. Why should it always be the other way round? As far as I am concerned, I will think twice before accepting your proposal." She rose from the steps to indicate that the interview was over.

Rajesh did not know how to slink away.

The next day, the classroom was abuzz when Meera entered.

"Congratulations, Madam; we want *mithai*," the students chorused merrily.

"What is this about?" she asked surprised.

"Madam, we hear an aspirant had come from Jammu to meet you. Has your marriage been settled?" Majid spoke.

"Let us start the lesson," she said curtly.

ฆ൫ฆ൫

But Meera lapsed into melancholy from that day. Her ebullience vanished. She lost interest in teaching. Her sleep and appetite became erratic. She had so many questions in her head that seemed to have no answers. Had young Kashmiri Pandits gone astray? How could they be so crude, callous, uncaring? Had they not learnt any lessons from history? Had exile taught them nothing? How could the Pandits claim to be intellectuals and liberated souls?

Meera did not explain the reasons for the fiasco to her parents. She thought it would hurt her mother to learn that her Doda origins had anything to do with the failure of the proposal. When they phoned she answered their questions briefly. Her worried father travelled to Kashmir to find her in a state of depression. He persuaded her to report sick at school and accompany him to Jammu for a change.

That is when she saw me the third time.

"I am sorry for what you have gone through," I commiserated after hearing her unsavoury experiences.

"It is better to stay a spinster than plunge into the dark pit of wedlock," she lamented.

"Look, every Pandit young man is not as dreadful as you might have come to believe."

"Three interviews have opened my eyes."

"It is they who are the losers, not you. Come on, put it all behind you and move on in life. There is a big world out there."

"But the world is a strange place; I am not being allowed to be myself. They seem obsessed with my marriage."

"Is it your parents?"

"Their concern is natural, but it is the students who are so intrusive."

"Do they know that the interviews didn't click?"

"They seem to get all the information. Sometimes I get a feeling there are sleuths stalking me."

"Did any of them broach this topic?"

"They did. Three weeks after the event, Majid, the boy who had ridiculed Ganesha as an elephant-headed, mouse-riding god, came to see me during the midday recess seeking guidance for a debate he was participating in. I think he was waiting for an opportunity to get even with me.

'Madam, we were sad to learn about the interview,' he said.

'What interview are you speaking about?' I asked him.

'The interview with the Jammu guy who had come to propose to you.'

'You needn't be sorry?'

'But you are one of our best teachers. We care about you and just can't believe you were rejected.'

'Why do you think I was rejected rather than the other way round?'

'Either way, the end result is the same, Madam. If you don't mind, will you now reconsider my sincere suggestion?'

'I don't get you.'

'About Mushtaq sir, the Urdu teacher. He is one of our best teachers and a gentleman par excellence.'

'So he is.'

'What about marrying him?'

"I reminded him that he was a student and not a matrimonial consultant. But he went on: 'What about Gani sir, the science teacher. Such a pious man, knows the *Koran* by heart, goes for *nimaz* five times a day. There are others who would consider it a privilege to win your hand.'

'You are crossing the line, Majid. I command you to

leave me alone.'

'I am sorry, but I have spoken in good faith.'

"He bowed respectfully and left. It was frustrating. I felt friendless, helpless. There was nobody to share my thoughts with. But I did not give vent to my inner turmoil and went about my job. A few days later, Aslam, the student who had asked me to convert, followed me as I was walking out of the school. Catching up, he said, '*Salaam* Madam, we are all concerned about you.'

'Why should you be concerned?'

'Because we have learnt about your failed interviews with the prospective Pandit grooms. Madam, don't you see sense in what I said the last time I met you?'

'Sense in what?'

'In accepting Islam.'

'You are being outrageous.'

'But Islam is a great religion.'

'To you your religion, and to me mine. Isn't that what Islam teaches?' I reminded him.

'It does, that is why I am asking you. What is your religion worth if you can't find a suitable husband,' he asked disdainfully. I was shocked.

'If young men from your community can't see the good in you, why don't you consider converting and marrying Mushtaq sir?' he continued.

"I warned him that if he persisted with his insinuations

I would report him to the principal."

'I am sorry if I sounded disrespectful, but that was not my intention; I said it all in good faith. Goodbye, Madam.'

"I was utterly distressed. Everyone was speaking in 'good faith'. What was this faith all about? Why should I be the target of this faith; why this unsolicited advice? Why couldn't my students leave me alone?"

Meera looked away in the distance, tapping her feet on the floor.

"Look, we can't escape the society we live in. Students in that age group are generally inquisitive and irrepressible. Don't burden your mind with what they said," I empathised with her.

"Notwithstanding their unabashedly presumptuous behaviour?"

"Yes, that is somewhat discomfiting and makes me wonder if they are doing it on their own? What about your colleagues? Did the Urdu teacher, or any other colleague, ever propose directly or indirectly to you?"

"No, he did not, nor did any one else."

"Do you think he would like to?"

"I don't know."

"Did he throw any hints during a general conversation, or through gestures and actions?"

"I don't think he did."

"Could he have employed the students, now that two

of them have suggested his name to you?"

"Frankly, I can't say."

"How is their attitude towards you—I mean your colleagues?"

"On the whole, most of them are courteous as long as I abide by the unwritten laws of the land and weigh my words before I open my mouth. You see, politics and religion are like their life and soul. It is a daily challenge to face this obsession. I keep out of these domains; that is the best way to have cordial relations with anyone there."

"You are not at any point of time considering giving up your job and returning to Jammu?" I asked.

"I have to like my job even as I live in sufferance because there is little hope of getting anything equivalent in Jammu. My parents have worked hard to educate me and it is my turn to help them out in their advancing years."

"How long can you do it?"

"As long as it takes."

"Have you shut the doors on marriage?"

"Yes, for now."

"Are you angry with the young men from your own community?"

"I am not angry; I feel ashamed. Nothing seems to have changed since the times my father married a girl from Doda because no Pandit would give his daughter to a shopkeeper of modest means. But for her, he would have remained a bachelor and I would not have been born to suffer the humiliation that I do now."

"You sound very bitter."

"More than bitterness I feel sad about our prejudices, about the false values and demeaning practices that hold us in bondage. Is it fair to blame the younger generation who crave to break the shackles? Rather than trying to eliminate the rot within, our leaders and elders cry foul when young boys and girls marry outside the community." She heaved a long sigh that seemed one of relief after she had given vent to the thoughts that caused her anguish.

"If the Urdu teacher made a proposal, would you consider it?" I asked casually.

"I hope I don't have to."

There was an inscrutable look on her face as she rose from the chair to leave.

# Brush with a Terrorist

March and April 1990 saw militancy in Kashmir at its acme, epitomised by mindless violence and killing of people by the terrorists, massive processions and strikes, bomb blasts and long stretches of curfews. Spring was never as capricious as that year. It remained for long in the clutches of winter, which, like the militants, sharpened its cold and merciless fangs to sting deeper. The freakishness of the season was only matched by our moods which had been sinking from all-time lows to abysmal depths with the news of more and more abductions and killings of innocent Pandits, some of them well known to us. Our thoughts kept pace with the changing moods and attitudes. One moment we felt like taking the first flight out, the next moment our reason told us to persevere. It was hard, very hard and agonising to forsake the legacy of thousands of years and tear yourself away from your motherland that was the very core of your being.

It was during those days that I found a hand-delivered letter in our mail-box addressed to Leela, my gynaecologist wife. Handwritten in Urdu on a photocopied letterhead of Jammu and Kashmir Liberation Front, it ran thus: 'While we concede that you are a competent doctor, it has come to our notice that you have not reduced your consultation fees as per our directive to all the practicing doctors. We are constrained to appeal to your good sense and sisterly instincts to halve your fees forthwith, failing which, we warn you, we will not think twice in taking the extreme step.'

We didn't know what to make of the letter. Was it just to bully us or was it a harbinger of serious trouble? There were not many patients because of curfews and strikes. Most of them were Muslim and they felt grateful that we did not close our door to them in these difficult times. Besides, we never demanded fees from anyone even in normal times, and never accepted it from a patient who could not afford. Yet here was an extra-constitutional order, a writ that ruled the roost in those tumultuous years, which could not be taken lightly. Any other person receiving such a terse warning would have left the valley even without a second look at the letter but we decided to wait and watch.

However, the chill of fear stung deeper after the letter. Even the sound of a radio out of tune, of a cistern filling with water, of leaves rustling in the breeze — these everyday sounds — felt menacing at times. The ringing of our doorbell sent our hearts aflutter, a knock on the door and we took positions, a telephone ring and we wondered whether it was an unknown caller threatening us to take flight or face the consequences. We looked into the letterbox and our hands trembled while scanning the mail lest there was another letter or a warrant from one or the other terrorist organisations.

I had a fixed schedule — drop Leela at Lalla Ded Hospital at ten in the morning, drive down to SMHS hospital where I worked, attend to my patients, take ward rounds with the interns and house physicians, avoid any discussion on the crazy happenings and return at four in the afternoon to pick Leela en-route home.

We had been provided curfew passes to enable us to commute to the hospital and back. Most of our colleagues used the hospital ambulances. I preferred to drive in my car in spite of the risk it entailed, because the ambulances took a circuitous route picking doctors from their residences which wasted a couple of hours both coming and going.

It was one of those days when I had dropped Leela at her hospital that two young men appeared as if from nowhere and forced their way into my car. I shuddered with fear even though they did not look out of the ordinary or menacing.

"Please don't be frightened. You won't be harmed as long as you do what we say," one of them said politely. He was gruff-voiced, short and stocky.

"Look, I am a doctor; I am in a hurry to reach SMHS hospital. My patients are waiting," I pleaded.

"We know you are a doctor; that's why we are here."

"Please get out of my car."

"Don't argue, just drive on as we tell you," snarled the second one. He was taller, thinner, fairer, and sharper with his tongue.

"I am not moving from here," I remonstrated.

"Don't try our patience, doctor. We have been nice to you; you wouldn't want to make us angry, would you? Take the return route; the same which you take when you drive back to your home. If you are stopped by the police, show your identity card. Remember, we are your assistants in your private clinic. Right?"

"Right," I replied as I realised that they knew everything about me and my routine.

"Think of your family before you make a wrong move. Okay?"

"Okay," I said mechanically as it dawned on me that I was being kidnapped. I could not even bring myself to imagine how it would end. Were they going to put ransom on my release, or use me as an exchange for their comrades in detention, or eliminate me? But I worried more about my family — my wife and daughters. What would Leela do when I failed to turn up to pick her from her hospital? How would my daughters take the news? How would they carry on without me in these difficult times?

We drove towards the bund. My van, which stood out during those days of scanty traffic because of its red colour, was familiar to the security personnel at different check posts on my way to and from the hospital. They knew by now that I was a doctor.

Srinagar city had transformed into a veritable cantonment. Military bunkers fortified with sandbags were in evidence at important squares and crossings. The long barrels of guns spiked menacingly from the small openings in the security pickets. Bridges and public buildings, the special targets of the militants, were heavily guarded. It was a war-like atmosphere. A pall of fear hung everywhere.

And now, as I drove my van with the two strangers breathing down my neck, fear robbed me of all logical thought. How could there be reason in this age of unreason and madness that had gripped the city? For a moment it occurred to me to stop near a check post and hand them over to the police, rush back to pick Leela, go home and pickup my daughters and take my family out of the valley before anyone knew or before the terrorists retaliated.

I found myself driving on the Zero Bridge. On my right, the Shankarachraya Temple stood towering over the city, gazing down at the macabre scene below. By some reflex, I slowed down for an intimate look at the temple where I would pay my obeisance every morning before I started my day, a climb that had not been possible since terror was unleashed in the city and it was dangerous to venture out alone on the heights: I took a deep breath and felt the benevolent hand of the Lord on me. Strangely, my fear abated and I asked the first question: "What is this all about?"

"You are going to examine a patient," said the gruff voice.

Somewhat relieved, I gathered the courage to protest again, "I will be late for my work. I could do it after hospital hours."

"Well, our commander can't wait. He is tossing and turning with pain; it could be serious."

"In that case, you should shift him to the hospital and I will do all I can."

"No, he can't go there."

"Why not? These are curfew days and shops remain shut most of the time. How will you procure the drugs that I might prescribe?"

"You needn't concern yourself with that. We will arrange whatever you prescribe."

Near Sonwar I was asked to slow down and stop at the mouth of a side street. The tall man took the keys of the car; the gruff voice produced a bandana from his pocket and started blindfolding me.

I raised my hand to stop him. "That won't be necessary. I will not speak to anyone about this."

"It *is* necessary," his voice became gruffer.

I lowered my head slightly to let him tie the band over my eyes. He helped me out of the car and we started walking together. He held my hand, prompting me from time to time to turn right or left as if we were going through a maze, cautioning me to mind a ditch or a pothole here, a hump or a mound there. It is incredible how in normal times we traverse these lanes without realising the pitfalls, as if we could do so with our eyes shut. But now, with a blindfold, it was like walking in a void without any direction. There were numerous drains that cut across the lanes, reminding me how primitive our drainage system was even in the twenty-first century, and how we accepted it without complaining. If a fraction of the expenditure on counter-terrorism were to be spent on these basic civic amenities it would transform Kashmir. I was lost in these thoughts when I stumbled against a stone and almost fell down. Luckily my companion held me fast.

I repeated my request to be relieved of the blindfold but not before I had walked for nearly fifteen minutes. We had done so many about-turns that, by the time we reached our destination and he removed my blindfold, I felt sure I had been led back to a place not far from where I had stopped my car.

It was a blind alley. I looked around, feeling dwarfed by the tightly packed houses with overflowing balconies and sky-touching attics. We passed through a door in the mud wall on the left to find ourselves in a small front yard filled with a crowd murmuring to each other. A hush descended as their eyes turned on me. One of them must have recognised me for I saw a woman nudging another, whispering my name in her ear. A group of young bearded men in *pherons* and skullcaps stood guard at the main porch. They parted to let me in. I was led inside the house and onto a backroom in the first floor.

On a large bed, the bearded commander in a shalwar, shirt and waistcoat was bent forwards, clutching and pressing his right flank with both his hands, a low groan escaping his lips. He must have been about thirty. A young man was holding his head and another rubbing his shoulders gently to ease his pain. He seemed like a caged lion. I was startled to see my doctor's bag on a side table but soon realised that the tall man must have carried it from my car.

"*Namaskar mahara,*" the commander uttered like a child. I was surprised at that address when I expected *asalaam alekum* or *adab*, or a haughty nod or cold indifference. The terrorists had enforced a strictly Islamic code of conduct in all their transactions including dress and speech, but here was their leader using a typically respectful Kashmiri Pandit address. It did not seem deliberate but out of a habit acquired from a long tradition. You can't easily wish away or wash away from your mind the common social nuances and practices in spite of the diktats that you might yourself have authored.

Disarmed by that unexpected welcome, I responded with a *Namaskar*.

"Sorry to have bothered you but it could not be helped."

"It is all right. Let me know the full story."

"Story?" He looked from me to his assistants and back. Possibly he thought I was asking him about his militant activities.

"I mean about your illness."

The tall man who had taken the car keys from me spoke for him. "Doctor Sahib, he has been in severe pain for two days. We got him a local doctor. He suspected appendicitis, whatever that means. He said he can't take the risk of treating this condition which needs immediate surgery. You see, our commander can't go to the hospital; the police are looking for him. You are a well-known physician; that is why we had to lift you. You will have to get him well without surgery. We will reward you amply."

For the first time in my life I wished I were anonymous rather than 'well-known'.

"Look, Mr… I seek no rewards. You got me here while my patients are waiting. You are not serving the cause of the common man that you claim to do by forcibly 'lifting' people." I don't know how I gathered the courage to reprimand him in the presence of half-a-dozen young men in that room, all in their twenties, two of them armed with Kalashnikovs. No one spoke. For a moment I felt I had the upper hand.

The commander took over and, in spite of his pain, gave a lucid description of a typical renal colic. He had been getting repeated colic for two days. He had passed pink urine the previous evening. There had been no other urinary symptoms, fever, or vomiting. He had never had any major illness or colic in the past.

On examination, he didn't have fever, his vital signs were normal, his right renal angle hurt on gentle thumping. The abdomen was soft and non-tender. His bowel sounds were normal. There was no suggestion of appendicitis.

"There is good news and there is bad news," I declared.

The patient stopped groaning, looking rather perplexed. His comrades looked uncertainly from me to their commander.

I wrote out a prescription for an antispasmodic-analgesic injection and tablets and handed it over to the tall man. "Can you get these from somewhere?"

"Yes, there is a chemist in the neighbourhood; it will take me a couple of minutes," he said and rushed out.

"Tell us the good news doctor," asked the gruff voice eagerly.

I addressed the commander, "I don't think you have appendicitis, so you don't need to go to the hospital as of now."

They heaved a collective sigh of relief, looked up at the ceiling and raised their hands in gratitude to the almighty.

The commander gave a wide grin even as he resumed swaying his body to and fro to subdue his pain. "Thank you, Doctor Sahib. I don't care about the pain. I can take bullets; pain is a small thing. But I don't want to go to the hospital. It is an abattoir. The doctors are butchers. Let me get well and we will teach them a lesson, *Inshallah*!" His voice had suddenly transformed and assumed a supercilious tone. Was he trying to reassert himself after having been humbled by the pain?

But I wouldn't let him off the hook. "You are right. The atmosphere in the hospital is chaotic and scary. All routine has gone haywire. There are no students. Doctors and paramedics arrive late, leave early, or miss duty altogether. There is no one to ask questions, no accountability whatsoever. The wards are like fish markets; there is no control on the mobs that accompany the militants wounded in action, or with civilians caught in crossfire. They barge into the outpatients, the wards and the operation theatres without any fear or compunction, rough up the staff, manhandle the doctors, break hospital machinery, raise slogans of *jihad* and *azadi* and threaten the doctors and administrators. Have you ever considered who is responsible for making the hospital an abattoir?"

There was a long silence, as if I was speaking to statues. I thought I felt one of the Kalashnikov-toting men tightening his finger on the trigger. A chill ran down my spine and I could hear my heart beat in my chest. Luckily, the tall man returned with the injections just then. I quickly filled a syringe and gave the commander an intravenous shot.

I didn't betray my nervousness. The face off ended.

"What is the bad news?" asked the gruff voice again.

"The bad news is that, in all probability, it is a stone in the kidney which is trying to pass out. In the process it is causing pain."

"But you can handle that, can't you?"

"It is not difficult to treat the pain. The injection should take effect anytime now."

"What about the stone?" the tall man asked.

I addressed the commander. "It may pass out itself—depends on how big it is and where it is lodged. But that does not entail hospitalisation, not immediately. It could wait until you are better placed vis-à-vis the police, or until you cease your operations!" Once again, I couldn't restrain myself.

He stared at me blankly. One of the men brought in a cup of *kehwa* and a *bagerkhani* that smelt fresh from the oven, and placed it on a table in front of me.

"Please share some *kehwa*," the commander broke his silence finally.

I excused myself and got up. Gruff voice came near to persuade me. "It will please our commander."

I sat down again and started sipping.

Suddenly the commander sat up bolt upright in the bed for the first time since I had arrived and spoke animatedly, "I can't believe it; the pain is gone, just some soreness left now." He took my hand in his and shook it vigorously, "Thank you, *jenab*; many thanks."

"You might need the injection again if the pain recurs. Meanwhile, you should drink lots of water and tea."

I got up to go.

The commander eyed the gruff voice, called him near and whispered in his ear, "Pay Doctor Sahib his fees."

"That won't be necessary," I said.

"But you must get your wages," he said ingratiatingly. A faint smile played on his lips.

"I have decided to treat patients free after my wife got a threatening letter from JKLF. I don't know if that is your organisation."

His smile faded away.

"However, we don't expect doctors to make free home visits. We are not blind to the fact that this is your profession, your livelihood. We don't want to lose good doctors."

"You are not going to retain them by your methods,"

I said gently.

The commander assumed a thoughtful expression; the others looked at him curiously,

"See the doctor to his car," he ordered the two men who had 'lifted' me. Then, he addressed me amiably, "If there is anything I can do…. My men will be in touch with you."

"I hope that won't be necessary." I meant it from the depth of my heart.

"Thank you for taking the trouble. I hope no one comes to know of your visit here."

"You don't have to tell me. First, there is professional ethics that obligates us not to refuse our services even to our enemies. Second, there is what we call patient confidentiality by virtue of which a patient is a sacred trust with us and we don't divulge information about him to anyone."

As an after thought I added, "I wonder if you are ever guided by some ethics in the discharge of you activities. I mean is there anything sacred to you beyond the violence that you have unleashed?"

It was reckless on my part to say so but fear had vanished from my mind and for a moment I didn't care about the consequences.

They were shocked at my audacity and looked from me to the commander, but he remained silent and stoic. As I moved towards the door he ordered the gruff voice to spare me the blindfold.

I walked back with the two men, one on either side, the tall man carrying my bag and smoking a cigarette, the gruff voice speaking jocularly as if we had known each other for ages. We traversed easily the narrow lanes that looked narrower because of the houses woven together like cobwebs. It looked a totally alien place, as if it existed somewhere far from my own world. Soon we were back to where I had stopped my car. I was right in my guess that I was in fact in my own neighbourhood, in the bowels of Sonwar, the backyard, so to speak, of Indira Nagar where I lived!

# The Spit

He sat on the edge of the chair, his body leaning awkwardly, his eyes looking at me searchingly as if wanting to ascertain if he could trust me. I knew that expression from my long experience with patients who were in intense mental turmoil.

I smiled and waited for him to begin, but he hesitated, as if he had landed at the wrong place, as if he did not have the words to tell his story. He pulled out his handkerchief, wiped his face, and kept looking at me awkwardly.

"You are Romesh Bhat?" I prompted him.

He nodded.

"Well then, let me know your problem."

He continued to look at me, trying to find words. He was around thirty-five, unshaven, wearing an old suede jacket over a crumpled trouser and shirt. Long strands of hair flowed down his neck and shoulders from under the rim of his cap.

"Go on," I said reassuringly. "What brings you here?"

"The spit," he exclaimed, and looked away.

I thought I had heard him wrong.

"Spit?"

"Yes, the spit that can't be washed away, no matter how hard I try." There was deep sadness in his voice; his face seemed to say more than the words.

"What is it all about, Romesh? Can you please explain?"

"He spat in my face," he replied, heaving a long tremulous sigh, wiping his face again.

"Who did it?"

"That brute of a man, my father-in-law."

"Why did he?"

"Because he was mad at his son for choosing his fiancée without his permission." The hurt look in his eyes was quite disconcerting.

"That is preposterous. Your father-in-law seems to have directed his ire at the wrong person."

He nodded his head.

"Why?" I asked.

"He believed that I encouraged his son."

"Did you?".

"No, I had no knowledge about his affair with the girl.

In fact, when he announced his decision to marry and I came to know that his father did not approve of her, I asked him to reconsider. But he said he wouldn't ditch his girlfriend at any cost. It would have been wrong on my part to interfere in his choice of a life partner."

"So there was a misunderstanding?"

"There was no misunderstanding. My father-in-law has never dared to stand up to his own son. I have always been the scapegoat for the son's misadventures. I would take his barbs lightly, even sportingly, believing it was wrong to confront the father of my wife. You see, we have been taught to respect elders, especially our parents, even if they treat us unfairly. Besides, he is an old man, a bit crazy. I put it down to his life of adversity. But I cannot bring myself to forget the utter humiliation this time."

"What exactly happened?"

"It happened in the presence of all the assembled guests during the betrothal ceremony of my brother-in-law. When the rings were being exchanged, everyone started cheering the couple except my father-in-law. I was sitting near him. He wore a grave expression throughout the ceremony. One of the guests came near and asked, 'Radha Krishan, why are you sitting aloof, looking glum? Come on, bless the couple; it is time for celebration.'

"'Celebration, my foot!' he shot back. 'I can't bless an event that doesn't have my approval.' Then, he pointed his finger at me, gave me an angry look, and continued, 'This man here is responsible for the disastrous choice of my son.' And before anyone could say anything, he brought up a huge, thick blob of phlegm deep from his throat with a loud rasping sound and spat directly in my face."

No sooner had he said it his eyes started twitching, he choked with emotion and could not go on.

I patted his arm reassuringly.

"The spit hit me in the face and splashed into my eyes, almost blinding me for a while." His eyes became misty and he wiped his face repeatedly, avoiding my gaze.

"Doctor Sahib, all my relatives and friends were witness to this terrible humiliation. I would have preferred death to this disgrace."

"It is a disgrace for your father-in-law, not you, Romesh."

"Please, can you give me something to sleep? I have not slept all these months."

"Are there other troubling thoughts?"

"There are no thoughts. There is only the spit. I carry the spit with me everywhere; I can't get rid of it. It has clung to me ever since."

"Come on, I don't see it. You know it is all in the mind."

"It is there; I feel it all the time; I can't bear it. I have lost everything because of it — my sleep, appetite, and interest in work. I try to avoid people because when anyone refers to the event I go into a panic—my heart starts palpitating and I sweat and faint."

"When did it happen?"

"Fifteenth October."

"That is more than three months?"

"Three months and five days. I can't function at home, or in my office. I am an accountant. When I open the files, I see the spit on the pages. My boss is annoyed with me; I am on the verge of losing my job. I have lost the desire to live!" He wore a pathetic expression — part pain, part self-loathing.

"What happened after Radha Krishan spat in your face?" I asked.

"Sorry, I want to forget it all. Can you give me something to erase the spit? Some medication so I sleep and wake up fresh the next morning. I have already seen two doctors; they prescribed sleeping pills that gave me nightmares and left me drowsy and restless the next day. I want something that will wash the spit from my face and its memory for ever. Please doctor, I can't go on; I will break down."

He was desperate and in no position to reveal the details of his terrible experience. It was a difficult case — one of obsession compounded by the symptoms of post-traumatic stress disorder and an element of depression. I wrote out a prescription for him.

"You need to get rid of your handkerchief and get out of the habit of wiping your face every time; you will have to erase the memory of the spit," I said in parting, and asked him to see me in two weeks.

ꕥ

I was not surprised when Romesh turned up after five days. There had been just a marginal improvement. He was still restless and wore the same mournful expression. As he sat in the chair, he wiped his face with the back of his hand. I frowned. He understood.

"I am sorry for this. I got rid of the handkerchief as you advised, but I can't help but wipe the spit from my face; I have to use my hand instead.

"Well, let me know how you are on other fronts. Did you sleep well?"

"I get a few fitful hours of sleep, but I am miserable for the whole day with the sensation on my face."

"Romesh, I know how you feel..." I empathised, "I need to know more about the unfortunate events that led to it. You will have to cooperate."

"I feel shattered but I will try my best."

"Let us go back to the betrothal ceremony. What happened after he spat in your face?"

"It was like a lightning bolt; I was stunned. A dead silence ensued. All eyes were on me. I tried to wipe the spit off my face with my handkerchief. But it was so thick and sticky that even when I had wiped it away, part of it stuck. I was still wondering how to face the situation when he brought up another big bolus and spat at me a second time, along with a volley of abuse in his garrulous voice. 'Take another, you ill-begotten son-of-a-bitch!' His red eyes turned wild! People gasped in horror."

"That is abominable!"

"It was the gravest humiliation ever heaped upon me."

"Did no one stop him, or raise an objection?"

"It happened so suddenly. Not one of the guests who watched this outrage moved or spoke a word. It was as if everyone was frozen except for a group of children playing in a corner. They thought it funny and burst into giggles that still echo in my ears. I stood up and went to the wash basin but could not wash the tenacious spit away. It had stuck to my face."

"Romesh, you have to realise that a spit is not something that will plaster onto the skin."

"But I feel it on my face all the time, like a sticky gelatinous sensation. I can't get rid of it, no matter how many times I wash or wipe my face. I carry a feeling of nausea with me everywhere; the smell of dirty phlegm hounds me when I sit down for my meals. I carry the spit onto the bed. As soon as I rest my head on the pillow I feel an irritation on my face right where he spat."

"Didn't your father-in-law apologise after the incident?"

He nodded his head. "Even if he had apologised, it was

not going to help."

"What about your wife? Has she not been of any help?"

"She couldn't have helped erase the spit."

"I mean, did she make any amends on behalf of her father?"

"Sir, how can someone make amends for another's crime?"

"You mean she did nothing?"

"She did not see her father in this horrible act. When she came to know, I was on my way out of the hotel while the guests were looking on in horror."

"Did she not stop you?"

"She ran after me, but I pushed her away, left the venue and took a taxi home. I left her even more dazed."

Romesh broke down for the first time. He held his head in his hands, lowered it onto his knees and wept like a child. It took me a long time to console him, but he continued to sob and sniffle. Finally, he stood up to leave. "Doctor Sahib, I can't go on; I will come another time. Could you give me something else that will make me forget it all…? Please?"

It was no use persisting with my inquiry. I augmented the anti-depressant medication, added a hypnotic to the regimen and asked him to report in a week.

Romesh reported back after nine days. He looked morose,

but not wretched.

"Doctor Sahib, I am sorry about the last time. I hope you are not angry with me," he said as he took his seat.

"Not at all. I hope you are feeling better. Did you sleep well?"

"Not really, but I have been able to sleep at a stretch for two to three hours since the last consultation."

"And the other symptoms?" I was treading cautiously.

"I can't wipe the spit away. You asked me to erase it from my thoughts, but it is stamped on the mind as it is on my face." Suddenly he retrieved his handkerchief from his pocket and started wiping his face and rubbing his right eye as if he were trying to remove a foreign body.

"You will hurt your eye," I warned him.

I had noticed in the previous interviews that he had a nervous twitch in his face and blinked his eyes with every sentence he spoke. Now it had got more pronounced.

"Romesh, is there something else troubling your mind? I mean besides the spit."

He sighed deeply and almost croaked with emotion as he spoke. "My wife – she was inconsolable. After I pushed her and left the venue that evening, she gathered the full details from the guests, faced her father, severely upbraided him for his lunatic outburst, swore that she would never see his face again, and left the party to follow me home. She was utterly devastated; her humiliation was more complete than mine.

She did not look me in the eye for days on end, as if it was she who had committed the offence. She tossed a picture of her father, which hung in our lobby, into the trash can. She never referred to the incident; never spoke the name of her father or other relatives. She lost interest in everything."

"That must have made it worse for you?"

"It did. She seemed dazed all the time."

"What about others in your home?"

"There is no one else."

"No kids?"

He heaved another sigh and nodded his head. "No kids. Even gods turn their heads away from unfortunate wretches like us."

"Did anyone visit you from your in-laws?"

"My brother-in-law turned up the morning after the incident. He looked quite downcast and apologised on behalf of his father. He touched my feet and that of his sister and begged her to pay them a visit, but she refused even to speak with him. The only words she spoke were when he took his leave: 'Tell father, if I am not dead before he is, I will visit to perform his last rites, but never before that.'"

I went on to comfort him. "I feel enough amends have been made. Your brother-in-law apologised. Your wife has shown great character; she has stood by you."

"I wonder how she came to be born to this brute! I endured all the crudeness of my father-in-law because of her.

But the spit was the turning point. It just unhinged our lives. And I cannot forgive myself for having pushed her that day."

"Come on, that was a normal reaction. You need to talk it over with your wife and tell her that you have forgiven her father. That might help her, and you. Forgiveness is a great virtue."

His face turned pale, his eyes blinked fast, the nervous twitch returned and his chest heaved. "It is too late; everything has changed. I am ruined."

"You said your father-in-law is a crazy old man. You need not destroy your life for his stupid act."

"It hurts deeply when I consider all I have done for the family. There was a time when my in-laws were on the verge of destitution; I helped them out of the crisis. I would even buy cigarettes and gifts for my irascible father-in-law."

"Why did your father-in-law refuse to approve the girl his son had selected for himself? Was there anything seriously objectionable about her?"

"I didn't see anything wrong in her. In fact, she is quite a good person. I feel my father-in-law felt let down because his son went against his wishes. He whined that the girl was from a family beneath their status."

"But you said your in-laws were poor…"

"That is so, but even the poor have levels— the poor from a high background and the poor from a mean background; the new poor and the old poor; the average poor and the poorest poor. It is farcical, bizarre, insane! Isn't it enough misfortune to be born poor, than to have to also worry about the pedigree, class and caste? In any case, I had nothing to do with my brother-in-law's choice. The fact is my father-in-law wanted to vent his spleen on someone. His son does not take any nonsense from him. So he found me the easy target because I let myself become one."

"My dear Romesh, even gods have been humiliated by their fathers-in-law," I joked, trying to inject a light-hearted note into the conversation.

"I know how lord Shiva punished Daksh Prajapati, his father-in-law, for his insolence. But even if I were to decapitate the head of my father-in-law like Shiva did, it would not erase the spit from my face," he spoke with vehemence.

"You know the story then?" I continued in a jovial vein.

"Yes I know that lord Shiva was humiliated by Daksh Prajapati, the father of his consort, Sati. But the analogy with my case stops there. While Daksh Prajapati slandered Shiva because he believed him to be a disreputable god, my father-in-law spat in my face because I had always tried to be *good* to him!"

"Well, Daksh Prajapati was punished for his outrage. Do you seek similar reparation?"

"Then what would be the difference between gods and humans?"

"I understand your sarcasm about gods, but Shiva was enraged because Sati plunged into the sacrificial fire for she could not take the humiliation that her father had heaped upon her husband. *That* was an extreme provocation for Shiva."

"But Shiva got his consort back," he reminded me.

"In her new incarnation when she was reborn as Parvati," I corrected him.

"Doctor Sahib, pray tell me, how do I get my wife back? She is no goddess, nor will she be reincarnated."

I felt a current passing through my frame. What did he mean? Had he gone through a greater tragedy than the shame over the spit?

"What about your wife? Is she ...?"

A dark cloud of sadness settled on his face. His voice went feeble, the words coming with difficulty: "My wife... she died of the shame that her father caused her by spitting at her husband. There was no ceremonial fire she could jump into like Sati, but there was the river."

Romesh left me aghast. I had no more questions to ask him. I was left with the unenviable task of finding a way out to wash him clean of the spit and its terrible consequences.

# A Nick in the Windpipe

I picked up the receiver for an incoming long-distance call. It was Aditya, my 8-year-old grandson from California.

"*Nanu*, I choked yesterday!"

It took me a few moments to grasp what he was saying.

"What did you say, Aditya?" I asked.

"I choked; I mean, I *nearly* did."

Aditya always chooses his words carefully, deliberately.

"How did that happen? What did you choke on?"

"A piece of meat. But I coughed it out immediately."

"It could have been bad."

"Yes, but Mom would have performed the Heimlich Manoeuvre. Even I could have done it on myself."

"Do you know how to perform the Heimlich Manoeuvre?"

"Yes, I do."

And he went on to describe the basics, fairly accurately, even though he revealed that he had learnt about it from his classmate who had done a project on the manoeuvre in the second grade!

Aditya's phone call sent me hurtling down memory lane, nearly five decades back.

The year was 1964, the month June, the place SMHS Hospital, Srinagar. I had finished my one-year house job and was temporarily posted as a casualty medical officer waiting for a rural posting.

If you had visited the casualty department of SMHS Hospital of those days, you would have come across a bare, drab, dimly-lit room with not much to work with. Yes, you would have found a ramshackle table, a stool and a chair, a few cupboards with scant dressing material, some bottles of antiseptics including the staple tincture of iodine, a stomach tube, and a few first-aid drugs. The common problems we faced in Casualty were fevers, headaches and body aches, all disposed of with aspirin. Serious medical problems and acute surgical emergencies were referred to the wards; women in labour sent to the delivery room. Dog bites and minor wounds and cuts were cleaned, stitched and dressed, depending on the availability of needles, thread and sterile dressings, which were generally scarce. In short, a Casualty posting was a sheer waste of precious time and largely irrelevant for a doctor aspiring to perform.

It was in this setting that I found myself one evening when a small group of people rushed inside and placed a boy of about six on the examination table.

"Doctor Sahib, please do something, please save this child," they urged in distressed voices. They crowded around the table, allowing me hardly any space for a proper look at the boy.

"Can you please give me some room so I can examine him?"

"Move back," one of them shouted.

"This boy was fine until a few minutes back, playing in the yard with other children. They were eating plums. Then another kid ran inside to inform us that he was coughing and unable to breathe. We rushed out to find him choking—he couldn't breathe or speak! We lost no time…."

The boy was semiconscious and turning blue. His face was bathed in sweat; his chest retracted with each frantic and futile attempt at breathing. The pulse was feeble yet fast. I looked inside his mouth; nothing there. It was obvious that his respiratory passage was blocked — most likely by the plum seed stuck somewhere in the windpipe — and that he was asphyxiated. I had never encountered a case like this and had no idea how to deal with this emergency in the setting of our casualty department. I knew that time was of the essence — the brain can tolerate oxygen deprivation for five to six minutes at the most. No surgeon could make it to the hospital in such a short time and remove the obstruction, but a call was sent all the same to the ENT surgeon, Dr Kosgar.

"A plum seed is blocking this boy's wind pipe and it is deep down where I cannot reach. I have no wherewithal to remove it," I said helplessly, throwing up my hands.

"For God's sake, do something; he is the only child of his parents," one of them pleaded, pointing towards the boy's father who looked at me with an agonised expression. I was shaken by that look of desperate entreaty.

What a shame that I had not learnt to perform an emergency tracheotomy, which meant making an opening in the windpipe to restore the breathing immediately. I was only a trainee and had just completed my house job in medicine. I had not even performed a minor surgical operation on my own. And the Heimlich Manoeuvre which my grandson spoke about was unknown then.

I suddenly realised how woefully deficient our training in emergency medicine had been and how insufficiently I was equipped to deal with emergencies in the Casualty. My shame only steeled my resolve to save the child.

"There is only one way out. One has to cut an opening in his throat to let the air into the lungs," I explained without wasting any time.

"Please go ahead; do whatever is necessary to save his life."

"But I have not performed, nor watched this procedure before. All the same, I will try, but please don't hold me responsible if he does not make it."

They were not interested in my deficiencies; they only wanted me to do anything that might save the boy's life.

"Certainly not," said one of them, "but we will be very disappointed if you do nothing."

I asked the medical assistant to give me the scalpel. From a cupboard, he quickly fished out an old scalpel which had possibly never been used. There was no time to sterilise it, for, by then, the boy had turned deep blue, his pulse had stopped and he was in a coma. I listened to his heartbeat. There was none. I threw the scalpel down on the table.

"I am sorry, his heart has stopped," I said in despair. "I can't cut open a dead boy's throat!"

There was a grim silence in the room. The men were stupefied. It seemed an eternity before the janitor on duty picked up the scalpel and thrust it back in my hand.

"Please take heart, Doctor Sahib. Take God's name and use this knife to put life back into this child."

He looked and sounded like a sage. This declaration of faith, coming from a menial, nudged me into action regardless of the consequences. As I moved to make an incision in the throat, the men who had brought the child to the hospital moved away from the table and stood with their backs to the wall, facing me and the boy. They extended their arms, their palms turned upwards towards the ceiling in prayer, their gaze fixed on the Almighty beyond. I looked at them before I plunged the knife — one fleeting look at their fervent faces, their cupped hands, their intense looks invoking divine intervention.

In one sharp sweep of the knife, I cut across the middle of the throat just below the Adam's apple. What followed seemed like a miracle! With a long swishing sound that still rings in my ears after so many years, a huge gush of air went in through the nick I had made in the windpipe, as if all the air of the world was waiting to fill the vacuum in the lungs of the boy. His chest expanded at once, and I pushed a rubber tube a couple of inches down into the windpipe. All at once, he started breathing regularly through the tube. His colour changed, as if by magic, from deep blue to pink in a couple of minutes. I thumped the child's breastbone a couple of times. His heart started beating again.

Suddenly, I was aware of the mess I had created — blood squirting from the cut, pooling on the patient's neck and breast, soaking his shirt; my bare hands bloody and sticky with the red fluid. I packed the wound with gauze and cotton wool, and applied pressure to stop the bleeding. Fresh sterile gauze was brought from the operation theatre, the wound was stitched, the mess cleaned up. The boy did not even wince in spite of the fact that I had no time to use a local anaesthetic. He opened his eyes as if from a frightful dream and made an attempt to speak. He was speechless from the seed that still blocked his windpipe above the nick I had created. Life was saved, speech would return later.

There was jubilation all round. The men hugged me; some touched my feet, others kissed my blood smeared hands, while others said I was a messiah. Everyone thanked Allah.

Dr Kosgar arrived much after we had shifted the boy to the ward. Since the emergency had been tackled, he decided to let the boy rest for the night.

Next morning, he removed the seed through a bronchoscope and pulled out the rubber tubing that I had inserted into the windpipe. The boy started breathing naturally and found his speech again.

"Say thanks to the doctor," his father instructed him as I approached his bedside.

"Thanks," the boy said in a hoarse voice.

"I am sorry for this," I said pointing at his neck.

"Say, you saved my life," prompted the father.

"My life ..." the kid echoed.

It felt great to find the child speaking again.

Then, the father proudly produced a newspaper from his pocket. *A doctor's daring feat saves the life of a child*, ran the news on the front page in the local daily.

Unknown till then, I became famous for a day!

When Aditya phoned again the next weekend, I related to him my five-decade old adventure. He listened with rapt attention and asked why I had not tried the Heimlich Manoeuvre before I went for the scalpel. I said I did not know about it then; in fact, no one did. Dr Henry Heimlich had first described it in 1974 as an emergency technique for expelling foreign material blocking the trachea.

Why didn't I think about it when it was so simple, my grandson asked.

It took me a while before I replied: It needs special vision to see what others can't, to think when others close their minds, and to act when others just watch helplessly. It is the simple ideas that have changed the world, that have made scientific breakthroughs possible, that have made the difference between anonymity and immortality.

"You did a heroic job—you even got into the newspapers!" he consoled me, sensing my regret for not being the one to think about the manoeuvre before Heimlich did.

"It certainly was a great experience that taught me how someone's faith in you can motivate you to give your best, and how ordinary people, like the janitor in the Casualty, may sometimes inspire you to move from indecision to action," I told him.

# Baptism by Fire

It was a clear sunny spring day in 1968. After having finished the rounds of the male patients, we were walking along the corridor towards the female ward, when an eager-looking man, holding a prescription in his outstretched hand, squeezed his way through the crowd of waiting attendants and advanced towards Dr Ali Jan, the professor of medicine.

He addressed the doctor in an exceedingly plaintive voice, "Sir, three days back you examined my brother; he continues to be in the same state you saw him in. Could you please visit him again? Here is your prescription."

Dr Jan looked at the prescription and advised him to continue with the medication since it was too early for a second visit.

We entered the female ward.

Coming out from there nearly an hour later, we again found the man waiting impatiently, with an extremely mournful expression. Dr Jan walked on, the man at his heels, the prescription still in his hand, making an impassioned plea for his visit. We watched the scene in amusement as we prepared to disperse.

Suddenly, Dr Jan called me aside. "Would you please go with this man and examine his brother during the lunch break? The patient is in a semi-coma; I am suspecting a brain tumour. I don't think we can do much, but why don't you go and have a look." Then he addressed the man, "Dr Chowdhury here will examine your patient and report back to me."

This was the first time ever that Dr Jan had asked me to see one of his private patients, a rare honour he did not easily bestow on anyone. But was he just passing the buck? What purpose would my visit serve if the patient had a brain tumour? What was my role except to go through the ritual of examining the patient and putting my stamp on a death warrant already issued by a doctor whose word was considered final? Yes, at that time, brain tumour with coma signalled the end of the patient. There were no diagnostic aids beyond plain x-rays, and neurosurgery was non-existent in Kashmir. This did not seem a very exciting proposition to me. I had just started my practice and was making little headway. And now, here I was supposed to merely to confirm what my boss had declared – an incurable situation. Nevertheless, I took the call.

The man hired a *tonga*. Soon we were trotting along the Karan Nagar road towards Chotta Bazar, taking a left to Kanya Kadal. From there, we drove towards Habba Kadal. It was a picturesque scene — a pleasantly warm sun in an azure sky, people in *pherons* haggling for fish, fruit, vegetables and kitchenware on the pavement shops on either side of the road. The Vyeth was meandering along gently, unmindful of the brisk human activity on her banks. Puffs of gentle breeze blew as we crossed the bridge and proceeded towards Babapora, stopping right at the 'tail', as they called the place down the end of a narrow and long road. I was led to the first floor of a small house. And then to a room with an extension on to the *dabb*, a wooden balcony common in most houses in Kashmir. It was a neat and well-lit place with pictures of gods and goddesses on the walls, a couple of chairs, and a table cluttered with bottles of medicines, a steel jug and a glass of water.

Mohan Lal — that was the patient's name — lay on a mattress on the floor, bolstered with cushions on either side. There was a small crowd in the room. Some of those sitting around moved aside to make place for me. I knelt beside the patient and started examining him.

Middle-aged and of medium size, he seemed to be

staring vacantly at the ceiling with half-open eyes, unaware of the surroundings, and unresponsive to questions. His breathing was quiet and shallow; his limbs were stiff and he did not make any voluntary movements. I lifted his arm and let go. It sank gradually onto the bed. He withdrew his legs slowly when his soles were stroked, and reacted to a flashlight with a flicker of the eyelids. Beyond that, there were no abnormal signs.

The examination revealed little except that his body was stiff and he was in a stupor. I wrote down my findings and advised the attendants to continue with the medication prescribed by Dr Jan. I had nothing more to add except to advise them to change the patient's posture frequently in order to prevent bed sores. I found one thing striking however — he was able to swallow water and other fluids fed with a spoon, almost by reflex, without choking; but when the attendants tried purees and mashed food, he made no attempt to chew or swallow and the food collected in his mouth.

We rode back to the hospital and I went straight inside Dr Jan's room to report my findings.

"Status quo?" exclaimed the professor.

"Yes, sir," I replied. "However, there are no localising signs that would indicate where the tumour might be," I added.

"You don't always find them."

I nodded in agreement.

The patient's brother left after he was advised to continue with the same treatment, disappointment writ on his face.

Two days later, as we came out of the ward after the rounds, the man was waiting in the corridor yet again. With palms joined together, he implored Dr Jan to examine Mohan Lal just one more time, but the celebrated doctor hardly ever made home visits. He suggested another visit by me. The man looked quite dismayed, but did not muster the courage to say that he was not interested in *me* — that he wanted the great physician himself to see his patient. That alone would give Mohan Lal's family the satisfaction and the confidence that care-givers crave for. There was a lot to choose between an unknown doctor and the doyen of medicine.

Nor could I dare to refuse when my boss asked me to pay another visit to the patient.

And so we left—a reluctant doctor being led by a sceptical attendant to examine his patient. The *tonga* sped fast on the asphalt. I tried to open a dialogue with the man but found him rather reticent. After all, I was playing second fiddle to the main physician. Obviously, I had failed to earn his trust on my previous visit. As far as he was concerned, my second visit was a pointless exercise. But I was undaunted by his attitude and coaxed him for details about the patient and his family.

I found Mohan Lal in the same position in which I had left him two days earlier. He lay on the floor, facing the ceiling with somnolent eyes. There was no eye contact, no response to my questions. I tried in vain to arouse him with a gentle shake. He seemed more rigid in the body, more remote. Other than these observations, a review of the nervous system did not reveal anything new.

I had an uneasy feeling that something was amiss. The cardinal symptoms of a brain tumour — headache, vomiting, epilepsy, motor or sensory impairment, visual or hearing deficit, or loss of bladder and bowel control — were missing in this patient. There were no signs other than the fixed, rigid posture and stupor, nor was there any evidence of raised intra-cranial pressure. From all accounts, his clinical status had remained static for nearly ten days! Was my vision clouded because I had started with a bias—a diagnosis by the tallest man of medicine in town? Was I missing something?

All this flashed through my mind quickly as I rose to occupy the chair nearby while a lady proffered me a cup of tea. Before I could decline, another lady moved near, squatted near my feet and implored, "Please do something to save him. Look at his two daughters; they are to be wed this fall. His son is still in his teens. I shudder to imagine what will become of them if anything happens to him!"

It was a touching spectacle. I looked around at the anxious attendants assembled there — the pretty but careworn faces of the two girls, the frightened wife, the cheerless old mother and the fretful brother — all looking on with helpless resignation. The son must have been away at school.

Fiddling with the cup of tea in my hand, I started asking the patient's history in detail, probing for clues that might have escaped my attention, some information that might help in the diagnosis. In fact, some important facts did emerge. This man had worked as a salesman in a provision store until a month back. He had been behaving oddly at times much before his illness, and seemed withdrawn and apathetic for several days before he finally went into stupor.

"He has been in this state for ten days, unresponsive and unchanging, like a living corpse — stiff and immobile, except for the quiet heave of the chest that tells us that he still lives," said his agonised wife, as I sat in the chair, contemplating.

Her statement was compelling. There was this constancy in his condition as if time had stood still. And neither his history nor the examination of the nervous system suggested a brain tumour. Nor was there any evidence of a systemic disorder to explain his mental state. In fact, she had led me to a new train of thought and I pursued it further with my questions.

"Has any such thing happened in the past?" I asked her.

"I don't know if this is relevant; nearly twenty years back he was on duty in Patna. He was alone. One day, we received a telegram that was hospitalised in an unconscious state. We reached Patna four days later. By that time he had recovered. We did not get any details about his illness."

"Why was he in Patna?"

"He was in the army. After that episode, he was discharged from service. We were informed that he had been erratic in his job and his superiors had recommended premature retirement."

"Has he remained healthy since then?"

"More or less..." she replied rather uncertainly.

"What do you mean?"

"Well, after he returned from Patna, he was never the same. He seemed rather withdrawn, and behaved eccentrically at times. We attributed it to his discharge from the army. However, within a few months, he resumed life, took a private job, and never looked back."

The fog started to clear as the details of the history poured in, reinforcing my impression that we were not dealing with a brain tumour. Just then, bright sunlight invaded the room from the southern windows of the balcony, lifting the gloom inside the room — and, it seemed, the fog inside my mind. The dying person seemed to come alive! My heart raced with excitement.

"I feel Mohan Lal doesn't have a brain tumour," I declared.

Everyone's faces suddenly assumed an incredulous

expression — more a mixture of disbelief and scepticism, and less of relief and joy. Was I trying to humour them, or was I in earnest?

"Not a brain tumour? Then what does he suffer from?" The men craned their necks towards me; the women looked at the pictures of the deities on the wall in gratitude.

"Something eminently treatable," I replied.

They continued to look enquiringly at me.

"It is called catatonic stupor," I said. They seemed mystified by that strange-sounding term.

I had read about catatonic stupor long back during our short training in psychiatry in my undergraduate days. I had never seen a case, yet I was almost certain about my clinical impression.

"What does that mean?" the brother ventured to ask.

"It means a type of mental disorder we call schizophrenia. Your brother has obviously had an episode when he was in Patna. Possibly, he was discharged from the army because of this disorder. He seems to have relapsed now. If it is alright with you, I will admit him this coming Tuesday. That is our admission day. Meanwhile, I will prescribe another drug."

He was unconvinced.

"What about Dr Jan? Shouldn't we inform him before starting the new medication?" he asked.

"I will discuss the case with him."

He thanked me, but his expression seemed to say, 'Can

Dr Ali Jan ever be wrong?'

The patient's wife kissed my hands in gratitude.

"Please don't worry; we will try our very best. I am sure he will recover," I said reassuringly.

"*Tathasto* — so be it," she said, her eyes alight with hope, "you have given me a new lease of life. God bless you."

We got back on the waiting *tonga*. Mohan Lal's brother decided to share the back seat with me instead of sitting next to the driver in front. Now that I had become a harbinger of hope, his attitude changed from indifference to geniality and he started asking questions. I was wondering how the patient would respond to my treatment and wanted to be left alone with my thoughts. The streets were busy with pedestrians and shoppers, stray cows and mongrels, bicycles and *tongas*. Life in the valley was simple, replete with these wonderful images of animals and people going about their business as the river meandered along lazily, the mighty mountains standing guard. And here I was, just on the threshold of my professional career, wondering what the future had in store, excited about my first encounter with a problem case.

Dr Ali Jan was an astute clinician and an icon. I was lucky to be working with him. And here I was now, a novice in the profession, just cutting my teeth, about to confront a veteran — a David about to face the Goliath — to inform him that he might have missed a diagnosis. How would I stand up to this baptism by fire?

I entered his chamber with trepidation. He was finishing his lunch of roast chicken and salad.

"Well?" he exclaimed, a faint smile on his face, eyes shining behind his glasses.

I hesitated for a brief moment, not knowing how to put my thoughts into words.

"Any new signs?" he asked.

"Sir, I feel we are not dealing with a brain tumour..." I replied, looking him straight in the eye.

"In that case, what do you think?" he asked in his characteristic soft voice, unexcited, and surprisingly unsurprised.

"Catatonic stupor."

"You mean Dementia Praecox?" The versatile physician was well-equipped with the whole range of medical terminology.

"That is right, sir."

"Rather too old to suffer from it, don't you think? I believe he must be in his fifties?"

"He is fifty-two."

"Well?" he exclaimed with the characteristic jerk of his neck

"There is a past history, sir. He suffered a similar episode nearly twenty years back and was discharged from the army. Besides, there have been other subtle symptoms of schizophrenia."

He got up, washed his hands in the basin, picked the towel from the ring and, wiping his hands on it, turned to me, "In view of what you say, Catatonic Stupor seems a likely possibility. It is good you dug out the history. What did you advise them?"

"I asked them to bring the patient for admission on Tuesday. Meanwhile, I have prescribed chlorpromazine. I feel we might need to call Dr Khushoo from the Mental Hospital to have a look."

I took leave from my professor.

Tuesday brought a big surprise. I could not believe my eyes when I saw two attendants helping Mohan Lal toddle towards me in the Outpatients. He was conscious, but dull and confused. I conducted a quick examination. He was slow in responding to questions, his cognitive functions were still haywire. There was only mild stiffness now, while his sensory, motor and reflex examinations were normal as before. I directed him to the ward. We conducted a detailed interview the next day and got more facts about the history which confirmed the diagnosis of schizophrenia. We called in Dr Khushoo, who agreed with our impression. Electroconvulsive therapy was started. Mohan Lal recovered within a week. He was discharged on Chlorpromazine.

Dr Ali Jan was a man of few words, he did not make a big show of his appreciation, but I feel I grew in his estimation. There was a lot to learn over the two years I worked with him. He started referring neurology cases to me from his busy practice.

Mohan Lal continued to see me for several years. The psychiatric condition remained under control. He never relapsed into catatonia.

# A Pinch of Soil

*Reason is our soul's left hand; faith her right – John Donne*

It was the summer of 1968. I woke up one morning at the usual time. There was a pain in my right lower abdomen but I got on with the morning routine of brushing my teeth and shaving. The pain built up over the next twenty minutes and, by the time I had my shower, it had grown a lot worse. I lay down in bed again. By then, Leela, my wife, had woken up and found me in distress. I felt nauseous and the pain had become steady and severe. She gave me a quick examination and found tenderness in the right lower quadrant of my abdomen when she palpated deep. Her jaw fell and she gave me one of those 'you got it' looks.

She phoned our colleague, Dr Shankar Raina, who arrived soon after and subjected me to another examination. The tenderness was persistent, as was the pain. There were no other signs.

He sounded the alarm. "This looks like acute appendicitis; let us drive you to the hospital."

By the time we reached the hospital, most of the faculty had arrived. We did not have any special rooms for sick staff members. I shared my office space with another colleague while Leela had a whole room to herself. So she put me up in her own official chamber. It had an attached bathroom and accessories. Dr R N Sharma, a young FRCS, was the surgeon on call. He put me through yet another examination, then asked his staff to move me to the theatre for an appendectomy.

Routine blood and urine samples were taken. I was put under anaesthesia and my appendix was resected even before the test results arrived—you did not need any lab confirmation once you made a clinical diagnosis of appendicitis. It was safer to err and remove a healthy appendix on suspicion, than wait for it to rupture and cause peritonitis and other complications. After all, it is only an appendage with little use.

Dr Sharma was endowed with, what they call in Kashmir, 'golden hands'. My surgery was uneventful and I was soon moved back to Leela's room. As the effect of anaesthesia was wearing off, I transitioned through a strange twilight state and started muttering, giving vent to some repressed thoughts. I spared neither the state government nor the Dean of our college for having ignored my claim to promotion. Most of my subordinate staff and other colleagues had gathered in the room to inquire after me. Even as we were having a good laugh over my blabbering, the pain returned.

It was not the usual post-operative pain patients complain of after surgery—it was undeniably the same pain for which I had been subjected to an appendectomy. Dr Sharma advised an analgesic injection which relieved the pain and I slept for the rest of the day. Leela stayed by my side, watching over me. We had been married for two years and blessed with a baby girl whom I missed badly.

The same intense pain woke me up in the middle of the night. I asked the nurse to give me another analgesic shot and slept until morning, but the pain was back next day around noon. The surgeon came and examined me. Everything was normal — my pulse, blood pressure, temperature and respiration. I had passed urine and sipped water. There was no oozing or swelling at the operation site. My bowels were rather sluggish, but that was to be expected after abdominal surgery.

"Well it is one of those things, Dr Chowdhury; I am sure it will pass," the surgeon reassured me. Around thirty-five years old, tall, well-groomed, and one of the younger generation of surgeons in our fledgling medical college, Dr Sharma was a rather serious fellow, not given to talking much and hardly ever smiling.

"Was it an inflamed appendix?" I asked.

He gave me a sharp look and I shrank back—it was the look patients get from doctors when they ask too many questions.

"Why do you ask? Do you think I removed a normal appendix?" He seemed upset, possibly because he thought I did not trust his clinical judgment.

"Even if you did, it hardly matters. Nearly a quarter of all appendectomies are of normal appendices. Those are the statistics in the best of hospitals with the most experienced surgeons. I am only asking because my pain has returned. If it was a normal appendix, we could look for other causes of pain." I wanted to reason it out at the same time as I tried to put him at ease in the vain hope that it would diffuse the developing tension. But it only incensed him.

"I know the statistics, Dr Chowdhury. In any case, I think the tip of your appendix was inflamed."

A doctor is generally a difficult patient. Either he is too inquisitive or too acquiescent, too obsessive about his illness or too reckless. In either case, he suffers. Physicians and surgeons treating their colleagues or other members of the medical fraternity tend to become either too defensive or too inflexible for the same reasons. If I ever need to seek consultation for myself, I try not to reveal my identity, although you tend to give yourself away sooner or later.

"Was the appendix sent for histopathology?" I asked gingerly, after a pause.

"You know what our histopathology department is worth?" he retorted. "I have scant faith in their reports. Besides, what else would you suspect in an appendix beyond the usual inflammation?"

There was no denying that the medical college was still in its infancy. Some departments, especially histopathology and biochemistry, were woefully short of equipment and staff. We were still evolving.

"If there is no evidence of inflammation in the histopathology report, perhaps we could think of another reason for my recurrent pain. In any case," I said, trying to make it up with him, "I am sure the pain will go away, as you said."

"I hope so," he said curtly. I felt sorry for being insistent.

He left with a sardonic smile, and I knew I had earned his displeasure. It was not going to be easy between us from now on—after all, I was the patient and he the doctor.

Leela glared at me reprovingly. "Why did you have to argue with him?"

"Well, I can't help asking questions; every patient has that right! Besides, I am a doctor too."

"For God's sake, take it easy," she said, trying to calm

me down. "Let us reason it out ourselves. It could just be intestinal spasm that's not uncommon after abdominal surgery, and goes away sooner than later..."

However, that was not to be. The pain recurred in the evening just when my father-in-law, also a physician, came to see me. He added two new dimensions to the possible causes—an instrument or a swab left behind in my abdomen during surgery, or a wrong ligature causing an obstruction! We could, more or less, rule out the latter possibility, for my bowel movements were fine. But a swab left inside? Well, that would be a remote possibility. But the pain did not subside!

Another shot of analgesic-antispasmodic gave me temporary relief.

By now, the patients of Ward 11 knew of my presence in the office chamber of their attending gynaecologist. News passed around that I had developed a complication of sorts. Before long, the husband of one of Leela's patients sought permission to see me. He entered and sat on a stool by my side.

"Sir," he said respectfully, "My name is Jan Mohammed. My wife is here, waiting for Dr Leela to operate upon her. But we realise she won't be free while she attends to you. She is very compassionate and helpful to poor people like us. I came here to tell you that we are going to offer special prayers for you. *Inshallah*, you will recover soon." He sat for a while before taking my leave. His empathy was genuine.

The third morning saw me convulsed with another bout of pain. I rang the bell. The nurse appeared at once, Jan Mohammed in tow. He dragged the stool near the foot of my bed, took his seat, and started rubbing my soles gently while the nurse filled the syringe with the pain-killer. I withdrew my feet, but he would not give up.

"I hope you do not mind, but rubbing the soles takes the pain away. I have tried it before; it works," he said apologetically.

He was doing me a favour and being so humble about it that I let him continue.

The nurse gave me the shot. Meanwhile, Leela breezed in after her rounds. But her face fell when she heard of yet another bout of pain.

"Your pain is baffling. I am terribly worried… let me get hold of Dr Sharma."

Ignoring my plea to give it more time, she left and returned with the surgeon. He examined me and thought my bowel sounds were still sluggish. Blaming the antispasmodic shots that I had demanded from time to time to relieve my pain, he inferred that they may have caused a mild ileus—a sluggishness of the intestines—and ordered x-rays of my abdomen and a blood test. He also issued instructions that I should not be allowed solid food, and that no more pain-killing drugs be administered to me without his permission. He was upset that I was self-medicating.

But what of the pain if it recurred, I asked.

He would decide after he saw the x-ray and blood reports, he replied, and left in a huff.

The blood counts and the x-rays were normal. I was only allowed light tea and plain water. I slept well that night, even though I felt hungry. Early the next morning, Jan Mohammed sneaked into my room and started rubbing my soles again. He was happy to learn that my tests were normal and the night had passed without any pain. He kept me engaged in conversation, humouring me with little anecdotes of his life in the village. He hoped I would soon recover fully and return home, so my wife would be free to operate upon her own patients waiting for surgery.

I was toying with the idea of asking Dr Sharma to let me have a light breakfast, but decided to wait till the afternoon. At about 3 pm the pain returned. Dr Mohan Lal, our senior radiologist, came to see me. He was distressed to find me in pain.

"What about seeking another opinion from a senior surgeon?" he asked.

I dismissed the suggestion; I didn't want to annoy Dr Sharma further.

"Can you do me a favour, and arrange a couple of Baralgan ampoules for me. I want to have an injection now."

"Why, is it not available in the ward?"

"It is, but my surgeon will not let me have it," I answered

truthfully. "He has ordered a moratorium on antispasmodics because he suspects an ileus... I do not feel that I have developed ileus, nor that an occasional antispasmodic shot can cause it."

Mohan Lal was an elderly person, a father figure in the hospital, and a good friend. He went away to return with the ampoules. He administered one intravenously and sat by my side till I got relief.

"Why should your pain recur if it was just an appendix that has been removed? Have you considered other possibilities?"

"Other than the bouts of pain, I am perfectly well. I feel hungry, and there is no fever. My blood counts and X-ray abdomen are normal. I feel it could be from the kidneys, though it is not the typical loin-to-groin pain, it's localised in the right lower abdomen. And I have had no problem with urination before, during or after surgery. I feel it won't remain a mystery for too long."

After I woke up early on the fifth morning, Jan Mohammed was the first to enter my room. He pulled the stool near my bed and took his seat. He fished out a tiny packet from his waistcoat pocket, and offered it to me rather uncertainly.

I looked at him surprised.

"I hope you won't be annoyed. This is nothing but a bit of soil. If you swallow just a little bit, it might do you good."

"A bit of soil? You want me to eat that? Like an earthworm?" I asked, laughing to ease his tension.

"Sir, I assure you that it is clean, and sanctified too. I know you are a doctor and a man of science but this is a matter of faith." He sat near my feet and started rubbing my soles again, looking at me with compassion, innocence dripping from his face.

I did not know how to respond to his faith— that unique feeling which arises from deep within and brooks no argument. Either you have it or you don't.

"It may not produce a miracle, but it will do no harm," he went on.

I could not resist his impassioned plea. I took a pinch of the soil and put it on my tongue. It made him happy; his eyes shone with gratitude.

"*Inshallah*, you will get well soon!" he exclaimed.

Leela walked in while he was still there.

But the pinch of soil seemed to exercise a contrary effect—in no time, I started writhing in pain!

Jan Mohammed was pale with disappointment, a guilty look in his eyes.

During the previous night, I had thought out an algorithm in case the pain recurred. I put it into action now: I examined myself again. My abdomen was soft. There was no tenderness except at the incision site. I asked Leela to give me a shot of the spare ampoule of Baralgan that Dr Mohan

Lal had procured the previous day. The pain subsided in fifteen minutes. Next, I sent for a microscope from the lab, walked to the restroom, collected a sample of my urine, put a drop on a slide and looked under the microscope.

It was full of red blood cells! It was incredible—for four days, we had not performed a simple urine analysis! There is no doubt the first sample of urine before surgery had not shown any abnormality, but no one had thought of repeating the test.

What should have alarmed me normally came as a big relief, and I shouted like a child: "It is nothing but renal colic—possibly a stone struggling to pass! Come take a look!"

Leela peered into the microscope and grinned with relief. Jan Mohammed did not understand what was happening, but realising it was good news he was wide-eyed with excitement.

"I am hungry!" I declared. "Get me some breakfast, please."

By the time the toast was being made I felt a strong urge to urinate. I passed sand with the urine. It came out with a grating sensation. And that was the end of it!

Leela gave me a three-course dinner that evening. Next morning, Dr Sharma came on his routine visit. I reported normal, requested for a discharge, and thanked him for all he had done.

"I am glad the pain did not return. It was ileus after all," he said with great poise. Then he did something unusual; he winked and gave me a wide, winning smile. It looked so good on him!

I decided not to tell him about the recurrence of pain, about the sand I had passed; nor did I divulge the story of my transgressions—the clandestine antispasmodic Baralgan shots, and the three-course meal – and certainly nothing about the pinch of soil I ate!

When I reported back to work the following week, Jan Mohammed came down to my ward to inform me that his wife had been operated upon.

"It was a neat job. I am grateful to your wife," he said in effusive praise of Leela.

"Thank you for that pinch of soil, Jan Mohammed. Where did you obtain it from?" I asked.

"A holy man gave it to me."

"Can you please thank him on my behalf?"

"Do you think it did the trick, Doctor Sahib?" he asked eagerly.

"Well, it might have. Faith can move mountains. In my case, it had to move just a few tiny grains of sand!"

# Pain in the Face

*Pain:*

*The phantom stalks all the time*
*Now lurking in the shadows*
*Now in the mind*
*Now seizing hold*
*Inflicting itself on me*
*With unerring constancy*
*It cuts and tears*
*Burns and sears*
*Now forewarning*
*Now catching unawares*

1971: Robin, my elder brother, had arrived from Australia. Friends, relatives and neighbours came over to meet him.

We were basking in the afternoon sun of a late summer's day, sipping tea, savouring snacks... Robin had settled down in Wollongong, a small town nearly a hundred miles from Sydney. We were meeting after three years and listening with curiosity and amusement, as he narrated in his inimitable style, an engrossing account of his life about the mountains and the sea, the kookaburra and the kangaroo, the climate and the university where he taught soil mechanics.

There was a sudden distraction—a phone call.

It was from Dr TJ. She and I had spent a full year together in the same ward as residents in 1963-64, after which she had specialised in Anaesthesia and I graduated in Internal Medicine. Presently, we both were faculty members in our respective disciplines in the Srinagar Medical College.

Dr TJ was calling from the Government Nursing Home at Gupkar. This was regarding Mohamed Shaban, a patient who suffered from trigeminal neuralgia, a painful condition of the face. A day earlier, he had sought consultation from Dr Ali Jan, practising at the high profile Polo View. The legendry physician had sent him across the street to Dr PKS, directing him to inject absolute alcohol into the trigeminal nerve — the main source of the pain in this condition. Alcohol would knock off the nerve and stop the pain impulses.

Dr PKS was a well-known surgeon, but he had never treated a patient of trigeminal neuralgia, an essentially medical condition. Nor had he ever injected into the nerve. This was not his line, but a referral from the doyen of medicine was an order to be complied with, a challenge to be met, even as he had no idea how to go about it. Where, along the long course of the nerve, should he inject alcohol? When such a situation arises, doctors go back to text books and journals. Dr PKS asked the patient to report the following day to the Nursing Home at Gupkar, where he would administer the injection in the operation theatre, under aseptic conditions.

Back at home, he looked up the surgical 'bible'—Lee McGregor's 'Synopsis of Surgical Anatomy'—to recapture the surface anatomy of the nerve and to learn the procedure for the injection. It was all there, beautifully illustrated. But the procedure of injecting into the nerve, which lay deep inside the cranial cavity, seemed quite daunting. It called for lots of measurements and demarcations on the face and the temple to localise the nerve and its ganglion within the skull before one could direct the needle to the precise location. He did not feel up to the task, but since he had asked the patient to return the next day all the way from Tangmarg, it was a matter of prestige and commitment. He decided to seek the help of an anaesthetist. Anaesthetists are trained in giving nerve blocks during various operative procedures. That is how Dr TJ came into the picture.

"Dr TJ, there is a case for you," Dr PKS said to her on the phone.

"What is the case?"

"It is from God himself," he laughed.

"God?"

"Yes, the God of medicine, Dr Jan."

"Oh, Jan Sahib," she said with reverence, "well, I will be glad to.… "

"This is a case of trigeminal neuralgia."

"Where do I come in?"

"You will give the nerve block."

"Sorry, but I have never given a trigeminal nerve block," she informed him.

"You have to give it this time—for my sake."

"Do you have any idea how to go about it?"

"I have looked up Lee McGregor," he said, mustering up some confidence. "It seems a complicated procedure, but the two of us together should be able to manage."

The next day, Mohamed Shaban was ushered into the operation theatre and seated on the table. Dr PKS and Dr TJ started with the surface markings after consulting the 'bible', drawing lines on his head like draftsmen, using the measuring tape like tailors, and discussing the route and direction of the injecting needle like two prospectors drilling for oil. How deep the needle should go? And at what angle, in order to avoid injecting the alcohol into a wrong site? That could permanently damage a sensitive area of the brain! It was essentially a blind procedure and it seemed more difficult than opening the cranial cavity and injecting the nerve under direct vision.

Mohamed Shaban was perplexed—what were these doctors up to, marking points on his face and temple, debating all the while? Three years earlier, it had taken a doctor just a few minutes to give him the nerve block. And he had performed the procedure in his own chamber and not in an operation theatre. What was going on this time? What were they trying to figure out from the open book on the side table? He sensed that they were not sure about the procedure—that they were, in fact, wide off-course. He would not allow himself to be subjected to a wild adventure! He believed the redoubtable Dr Ali Jan would not err in referring him to the right person, but something seemed wrong somewhere. So he gathered up courage and spoke:

"Excuse me sir, excuse me madam, I would like to inform you that a young doctor working with Dr Ali Jan gave the first injection into my nerve three years back. It took him just a few minutes. It seemed so simple. He injected into my cheek and not in the temple where you are drawing the lines and taking measurements. When the pain returned this time, I went to Dr Jan again and reminded him about the injection his subordinate had given me last time… He could not recollect him, and that is why he referred me to you. When you called me to this nursing home – and since you are a surgeon – I was happy in the belief that you would perform a different procedure to give me a permanent cure."

His revelation sent the two doctors re-thinking. Were they off-track? Where had the previous doctor injected? Who could he have been?

"Which year was it?" Dr TJ asked him.

"1968."

"Did the doctor give you the injection in the hospital?"

"Yes, in his chamber in Ward 3."

"What did he look like, this doctor who gave you the nerve block?"

"He was young, of medium height, with curly hair and a receding hairline. Oh, he was a Pandit!"

That clinched it. I was the only Pandit doctor who had worked with Dr Jan in 1968. He had taken retirement later that year.

Dr TJ had a flash of recollection. "It is Dr Chowdhury. Let us call him."

That is when the phone rang. She explained her predicament and asked if I remembered the patient. Yes, I remembered having given the injection to a patient once, I told her.

"Would you do us a favour and help us out of this situation?" she pleaded. I said that my brother had just arrived from overseas and I offered to give her instructions on the phone. But she was not ready to try it on her own.

"I will request your brother to spare you for a while,"

she said, laughing.

I had no heart to disappoint a lady in distress. That would have been unchivalrous. And, if only for old time's sake and the many cups of tea we had shared, I could not say no. I excused myself, and left my brother with the fawning crowd around him. I asked him to save the best anecdotes till I returned.

Gupkar Nursing Home was just a couple of miles from my home. I was there in ten minutes. It was a small Victorian-style building in the foothills, with a tiny front-lawn and a beautiful rose bush in full bloom. Mohamed Shaban's face beamed with recognition and relief on seeing me. I remembered him well. He hailed from my favourite week-end retreat, Tangmarg – a pretty hamlet seven thousand feet above the sea on the way to the famous Gulmarg resort, the Ferozepur stream gushing down on one side and the dense pine forests flanking the other. Sometimes I wondered how the denizens of these celestial places — where fairies danced, angels sang and gods resided — could suffer such painful conditions. How could they die like ordinary mortals?

Mohamed Shaban was the only patient I had ever treated for this problem. Those were still early days in neurology and there were hardly any drugs for this painful condition. When phenobarbitone and phenytoin had given no relief, Dr Ali Jan had asked me to inject absolute alcohol into the nerve. I remembered that the patient had procured a vial from the department of chemistry of the S P College, since pharmacies did not carry it. I had injected it into the second division of the nerve. But peripheral nerves, unlike the neurons in the brain, have the potential to re-grow and re-innervate. There was always the likelihood of the facial pain coming back. Mohamed Shaban was now having a relapse after three pain-free years.

"Seeing you after a long time," I remarked, as he grasped my hand in gratitude for the previous service rendered and the service about to be provided.

A fur cap on his head, and a short waistcoat over a shirt and shalwar, he was around fifty. He was unshaven, his face contorted with spasms of pain which he was trying to smother with a swinging movement of his body.

"Thank you for coming, Doctor," he said, clutching my hand.

"It seems the pain is revisiting you?"

"Yes, it is. A most unwelcome visitor, I must say!"

"Since when?"

"After you gave me the injection last time, I did well for about two-and-a half-years. Then the pain started coming back – occasional short, sharp jabs to begin with, but over the next few months, getting worse and worse… Now it is very bad. Even a light touch causes me to wince; food in my mouth brings on severe pain, and chewing is out of the question. I cannot shave, I can't wash my face — even a soft breeze feels like a whiplash. It feels like burning, pricking and stabbing at different times. It comes and goes on its own and leaves me tired, sleepless, and depressed."

"Can you trace the painful area with your finger?" I asked.

Without touching his face, he pointed out the area between the eye and mouth, including the middle portion of the cheek, side of the nose, lower eyelid and the upper lip on the right side. This was the territory of the second division of the trigeminal nerve.

I tried to look for the trigger spots on his face by lightly touching and tapping in the specified area. It was painful. Every touch caused him to wince.

I turned to the two doctors. "Fortunately, his pain is confined to the second division of the nerve. It will suffice to block this division alone and not the whole nerve. We will inject alcohol into the infra-orbital foramen. That is what I did last time."

The infra-orbital foramen is a small opening in the bone on the face, and easy to locate. I marked it with a dot. I filled a syringe with one ml of a local anaesthetic, and another with a half ml of absolute alcohol. I directed the needle with the local anaesthetic from the point of entry into the tissues till it hit the bone. Then I moved the needle tip around and when I found the foramen, pushed the needle through and injected the local anaesthetic. With cotton-wool and a pin,

I confirmed that the area on the face under our scanner had become insensitive to touch and pinprick. That confirmed that the nerve had been anaesthetised. Leaving the needle in place, I now injected the alcohol from the second syringe. The procedure took me around twenty minutes.

"It was so simple." Dr TJ said with great relief.

"We were off-track because we did not examine him; nor did we take a detailed history." Dr PKS acknowledged with some regret.

"You were not entirely wrong," I reassured them. "What you were trying to locate was the main trunk of the nerve inside the skull. That is quite cumbersome, as you found out. If the whole face were involved in trigeminal neuralgia, it would be justified. But in this case, we had a simple solution since only the second division of the nerve is affected."

With the doctors' profuse thanks ringing in my ears, I hurried back to hear more of my brother's adventures.

But it was the patient who pronounced the last judgment when he came to my house a week later to say thanks: "When doctors do not know, they should be honest and say so, rather than make a patient suffer the consequences of their ignorance or lack of experience."

I agreed with him, yet there was more to the practice of medicine than the solving of a simple mathematical equation, I explained. It is a science that demands its practitioners to be equipped with a sound basis of knowledge and its correct application; an art that needs to be perfected through constant practice, innovation and experimentation It calls for determination, dedication and daring from the doctors, and patience, faith and sacrifice from the patients. The argument convinced him and he acknowledged that the two doctors were only trying to do their best — and in his interest.

Mohamed Shaban continued to see me. By the time he relapsed again in 1974, carbamezapine had become available for use in epilepsy. It worked wonders in trigeminal neuralgia as well, and I put him on the drug. He did not need any further injections. Out of gratitude, he would come down from Tangmarg every fall with a box of the best apples from his orchard that I really miss since I left the valley in 1990.

ജ്വര

# The Crux of Clinical Decision-Making

I was in the Outpatients department one Tuesday morning in the summer of 1971 when Mohammad Sultan was brought in, in a state of shock. The residents and postgraduate students started working on him. An hour later, when I joined them, they had gone through his history and completed the examination. They had set up an intravenous line and started resuscitative measures but were still fumbling for an answer to the cause of the shock.

The history was brief. This 46-year-old, short, stocky man had woken up fine that morning. He had walked halfway to the toilet and had been overwhelmed by a sudden wave of nausea that forced him to return to his bed. After some rest, he had made his way to the toilet again, only to feel giddy, and so weak that he slumped onto the floor. His wife had helped him to his bed. Soon after, he was brought to the hospital with acute weakness and sweating.

An examination showed telltale signs of shock. He was conscious, restless and apprehensive, pale and sweating profusely. His breathing was rapid, pulse fast and feeble, blood pressure low, and temperature subnormal. A full review of his systems did not reveal anything abnormal. There was no evidence of any rash on the skin, the lungs were clear, the heart sounds normal, the abdomen soft and non-tender.

A case of sudden onset of shock — what was the cause?

Mohammad Sultan was a milkman, a moderate hookah-smoker with no history of alcohol consumption or substance abuse. He lived an active life, tending to his livestock and delivering milk to homes every morning. There was no history of trauma, allergy or anaphylaxis, diabetes, hypertension, cardiac disease, arrhythmia, or abdominal pain. He had eaten dinner with his family the previous night. He had not taken any drugs in the recent past, never suffered any major illness, nor undergone any surgery. His bladder and bowel functions had been normal.

We ran the basic investigations and started infusing noradrenalin in dextrose and saline to raise his blood pressure. His urine analysis was normal. The white cell and platelet counts were within range. The haemoglobin and the packed cell volume (PCV) were both low at 10.5 and 32 respectively. Other biochemical parameters were normal. A chest x-ray revealed normal lung fields. The heart size was normal, and the electrocardiogram unremarkable.

We ordered blood and urine cultures.

By that time, the professor of medicine joined us on the rounds and we reviewed the case with him.

A run-through of the possible causes of shock — heart attack, severe sepsis, trauma, loss of fluids including external or internal bleeding, anaphylaxis, endocrine emergencies etc. — gave us no lead, and the facts and figures revealed nothing.

"Most likely, we are dealing with a heart attack, an acute myocardial infarction," the professor declared.

I argued against that possibility because there was no present or past history of chest pain, the ECG was normal, and there were no risk factors in the patient.

"But heart attacks can be painless and it may take some time to show changes in the ECG," he countered, and reminded us that the patient's smoking history was a definite risk factor.

I vouched for internal bleeding as the cause of shock in the patient, and put forth the reduced haemoglobin and low packed cell volume as evidence of blood loss.

He rejected that possibility. "That level of haemoglobin and packed cell volume is almost normal for Kashmiris, Dr

Chowdhury. Besides, examination of the abdomen in this case does not reveal any sign of a major internal bleed."

He ordered intravenous Heparin with the aim of dissolving the presumptive clot in the coronary artery responsible for the heart attack in our patient. This was the age of Heparin. There had been several reports in the medical journals of improved outcomes with Heparin in middle-aged males with heart attacks.

But if we were dealing with a case of internal bleeding, as I strongly suspected, it would be disastrous to administer Heparin — it could even prove fatal! We must wait and not rush with Heparin till the picture cleared in this patient, I argued. In any case, Heparin was not a life-saving drug in heart attacks; at best, it made a statistically marginal difference.

"Where do you suspect the bleeding, Dr Chowdhury?"

"Most likely … from a duodenal ulcer," I replied.

"But there is no previous or present history of ulcer in the patient. And he is rather old for a duodenal ulcer to present itself for the first time and with bleeding as the first symptom. Besides, it has to be a massive bleed to cause this degree of shock. It should have become manifest by now. He has neither vomited blood nor passed it in his stools. "

"I feel these will soon show up. It is not just a gut feeling, I can almost *smell* the blood," I said. Using statistics to bolster my claim, I went on: "It is not uncommon to see duodenal ulcers appearing in middle age with bleeding as the presenting symptom. Ulcer bleed is notorious as one of the most common causes of medical shock in the young and middle-aged Kashmiris, while heart attacks are uncommon, and painless heart attacks almost unheard of."

The professor had joined the institution just a few months earlier. Fresh from a long training programme in the USA, he was strong in theory but not yet fully conversant with the common emergencies in our part of the world. Heart attacks were no doubt on the rise in the west and a common cause of medical shock, but they were relatively rare in our setting.

He differed with my opinion, stating that it was several hours since the onset of shock in the patient and the bleeding should have become manifest by now. But he agreed to withhold Heparin for some time and directed the residents to send a sample of the patient's blood for cardiac enzymes testing (as evidence of a heart attack) and to run an ECG every hour to look for any changes.

"I feel we must arrange to transfuse a couple of units of blood in this patient. We may be losing time by withholding it," I suggested.

He disagreed.

A hierarchical medical system may have its strong points, but the chief's opinion always prevails even if it sounds frightfully wrong. I was worried about the patient but my hands were tied. I was an assistant professor and the second-in-command. All I could do was to direct the residents to monitor Mohammad Sultan's vital signs, watch for any evidence of manifest bleeding, and evaluate the haemoglobin and PCV levels every hour. Our labs were still primitive. While the report on cardiac enzymes would take a long time to come from the central laboratory, the other two tests could reliably and promptly be performed in the small laboratory attached to our ward.

Over the next hour, the patient stabilised somewhat. His sweating stopped and his pulse and blood pressure started improving. He passed urine but no stools. A repeat ECG did not register any change, but the haemoglobin level dropped to 9 and the PVC fell to 28. This was significant and I sent the chief resident to the professor's chamber with the new information. He was not impressed. A drop of one and half grams in haemoglobin was not significant in his view. He argued that the calorimetric method for measuring haemoglobin was subject to error.

Another hour passed; another ECG showed no change. The professor turned up after lunch to have another look at the patient. He was satisfied with the line of treatment, now that the patient seemed out of the woods. Suddenly, he renewed his advocacy for Heparin.

"It is no longer prudent to withhold anticoagulants," he declared, and directed the chief resident to administer 5,000 units of Heparin eight hourly to the patient.

I was aghast. "It will prove fatal in this case," I warned.

He sensed my irritation. "Come on, Dr Chowdhury, if the patient had bled it would have shown," he said persuasively.

"I am sure the bleeding will manifest anytime now," I replied rather brusquely. "The drop in haemoglobin and PCV point strongly to an ongoing bleed while a normal ECG even after six hours militates against a heart attack presenting as shock."

"Until we get credible evidence for an alternative diagnosis this is a heart attack, and we must approach the case accordingly," my senior declared with a finality that brooked no further argument.

It was like the judge striking his gavel.

I could accept a painless heart attack being considered as one of the possibilities in this patient even when the diagnosis of an internal bleed was staring at us. What incensed me was the intransigence about the administration of Heparin! The residents eyed each other as they found the two of us eyeball to eyeball. The professor left and I returned to my room to collect my thoughts.

What was going wrong in this case? Were we losing precious time? Were we missing some vital clues in the diagnosis, some life-saving steps in the management? And then it came in a flash. I had missed out on a simple diagnostic procedure to prove my point — that of passing a Ryle's tube down the food pipe into the stomach of the patient to find evidence of blood there. It was sad that hard posturing and confrontation had offset the sequence of logical thought and action. The tendency to close one's mind to possibilities and become fixated on one idea is the bane of medical practice, as much as the tendency to stick to one's gut feeling without doing anything to prove it.

I rushed to the patient. His wife was sitting by the bed, holding his hand.

"How is he doing?" I asked, as I held the patient's wrist to check his pulse.

Anxiety was writ large on the fair, round face of this chubby woman. She shrugged her shoulders in despair. "He does not seem well to me, Doctor Sahib. He is restless as you can see. I sent my brother to the market to buy the life-saving drug."

I did not understand which life-saving drug she was talking about. The nurse informed me that since Heparin was in short supply in the hospital the attendants had been directed to procure it from the market.

I heaved a sigh of relief. Providence seemed to be at work.

"Can you please get me a Ryle's tube?" I asked the nurse.

Meanwhile, I sat by the side of Mohammad Sultan to

feel his abdomen. He smelt awful, the typical fetid odour of blood in the stomach! His tummy looked fuller. It was soft but there was brisk gurgling. I placed my stethoscope on the abdomen and heard loud whooshing sounds that spoke of the rapid passage of intestinal contents.

"Would you like to move your bowels?" I asked.

He said he was passing a lot of malodorous flatus.

"Let us get you a bed pan," I suggested.

"No sir, I would like to go to the bathroom myself. My wife is here to help me."

I called the ward boy to fetch a wheelchair. But as soon as the patient was helped to a sitting position, he turned pale, felt giddy, broke into a sweat and swooned. As we lay him back on the bed, he lost control and passed a massive black motion — the characteristic tarry stool of an ulcer bleed — soiling his clothes and the bed sheets, enveloping the whole ward in a miasma of the offensive smell so unmistakable of an upper gastrointestinal bleed.

He looked deathly pale. His pulse was racing and the blood pressure dropped further. His wife looked on, wringing her hands. My heart went out to the couple, even as I was ecstatic that the suspense was over!

Yes, the cat was out of the bag! The bleeding had remained concealed for six hours— quite unusual, but not unknown. There was no need for the Ryle's tube now. I called the residents and dissuaded them from administering

Heparin, now that there was no doubt about the cause of shock. I asked them to arrange two units of blood for transfusion without further delay.

The chief resident came to my room a while later. He had phoned the professor and informed him about the black stools and asked if Heparin were to be given. The answer was an emphatic 'yes' for heparin and an equally emphatic 'no' for the blood transfusion!

I was furious! I warned him not to push Heparin under any circumstances, for that would surely kill the patient. He was caught between the devil and the deep sea.

"The professor will be angry with me, sir," he said.

"And I will be mad at you!" I retorted. "I want no Heparin given to this patient and that is an order."

I wrote the words NO HEPARIN on the case sheet of the patient and left the hospital in a sombre mood.

ജ ജ

Nobody in the realms of Medicine can claim immunity from making diagnostic errors. In the present case there were two probable diagnoses at presentation, but only for a while, until the haemorrhage became manifest. After that, there was no point in persisting with a wrong line of thought that would inevitably lead to a disastrous line of action. This was not the occasion to stand on prestige.

I did not receive any call from the hospital during the

night that passed in agitation and wild dreams. The next morning I walked into the ward with trepidation, not knowing whose instructions had been carried out by the residents and what turn this case had taken during the night.

The residents had struck a truce — they had neither transfused blood nor administered Heparin!

Time is a great healer, nature the best doctor. It is in the nature of a living organism to mobilise all its reserves and resources in the face of danger. That is what had happened in our patient. The bleeding had stopped, he had stabilised, and his vital signs had improved.

I don't know what must have transpired in the professor's mind during the night, but when he arrived for the rounds and saw the patient all smiles, he was elated. He grunted with satisfaction, and waxed eloquent on the usefulness of Heparin in acute myocardial infarction.

The residents looked uncomfortably at one another and I felt the onus was on me to explain.

"But the patient did not receive any Heparin," I said.

"What!" he exclaimed.

"Since the patient had a massive black motion, I did not allow Heparin. It would have had grave consequences in this situation."

"I don't believe this was an ulcer bleed." Surprisingly his tone was conciliatory; there was no sign of exasperation.

"We can't deny that he bled profusely. Nor can we deny

that the source of blood must have been somewhere high in the gut, most likely a duodenal ulcer. Nor that it was the blood loss and not a heart attack that caused shock," I reasoned.

"On the contrary, I believe he had a heart attack as the primary event, which led to shock, and the bleeding was a consequence of intestinal ischemia secondary to shock," he said smiling and nodding his head in self-affirmation.

This was quite a tortuous line of reasoning — a long shot, indeed! He was stretching the realm of possibilities to its most incredible limits and committing the mistake that should be avoided at all costs — making the diagnosis of an uncommon disease with an uncommon presentation and an uncommon complication, when a simpler alternative was staring us in the face.

I looked at him in utter disbelief. Even if one accepted the most unlikely possibility that shock was from a heart attack and the bleeding a result of ischemia of the gut from the shock, there was still no point persisting with Heparin. It would kill any one with bleeding from any source, whatever the cause. Even a layman would understand that.

I could not hide my impatience. "I see not a shred of evidence of a heart attack; the ECG has stayed normal for more than twenty-four hours. It must be the first ever reported case of a heart attack massive enough to result in shock so severe as to cause gut ischemia and haemorrhage, and yet not produce any changes in the ECG. Besides, he does not complain of abdominal pain which is the hallmark of ischemic colitis, and he has not passed the maroon red stool characteristic of ischemic colitis."

"Let us take another ECG. It may yet show the changes," he said in an uncertain tone, trying to catch at the last, loose straw.

An ECG was done while we all stood by with the patient looking on, feeling important at the attention that he was receiving, ignorant of the fierce debate that raged around him.

The professor held the ECG in his hands and peered at it keenly like an astrologer looking at a horoscope. Pulling out an ECG scale from the top left pocket of his white coat, he started explaining the 'changes' in the graph.

It was turning farcical. Strangely, my annoyance left me and I desisted from arguing any further. The professor did not mention the word Heparin again. Nor was there any further discussion on the case during the rounds in the following days.

Mohammad Sultan stabilised by the next day. He felt well enough to stand and walk. On the fifth day he asked for discharge, but the professor advised him to stay back for three weeks — that used to be the mandatory period of hospital stay for a heart attack patient. His ECG was taken every day, the professor going through the ritual of taking out his pen and ECG scale to look for the changes that never materialised. For the third time in succession the test for cardiac enzymes returned normal values.

The patient grew impatient with this routine that seemed as pointless to him as to me, and possibly to the rest of the staff. At his insistence, he was discharged on the tenth day. He had regained colour and looked fresh and even handsome in the fresh new clothing his wife had brought in. He received a discharge summary and was asked to come for a follow up. The professor saw to it that the diagnosis entered in the discharge summary was Acute Myocardial Infarction.

Mohammad Sultan must have had the last laugh; he never turned up for the follow-up. Instead, a week later, his wife came to distribute pieces of mutton to the nurses, ward boys and janitors of our ward. They had sacrificed a lamb in thanksgiving since he had fully recovered and resumed work.

# The Brigadier's Salute

I made the diagnosis the moment Hardayal Singh stepped into my consulting chamber. He was an elderly Sikh, around seventy, and slightly stooped. He walked with a slow, stiff, shuffling gait. He was accompanied by his son, a huge physical presence in a military uniform with three gold stars on his epaulettes that marked him as a brigadier.

Hardayal Singh related his story and answered my questions faithfully in a dull monotone, but the brigadier kept adding details and digressing — how he had gone from one doctor to another and the interactions with them, the long list of investigations, and his own interpretations — details that seemed superfluous to me. The patient complained mainly of pain and stiffness in the shoulders and legs for which he had consulted his family physician.

After treating him for several weeks, the physician had referred him to an orthopaedic surgeon. The latter had tried his armamentarium without much success. In turn, he had referred him to a rheumatologist who took his own time with a new set of investigations and then sent Hardayal Singh to a psychiatrist. By that time, the son had been transferred to Kashmir, and the patient was fed up visiting doctors.

It was obvious the doctors were quite off the mark. They had been treating him empirically for frozen shoulders, rheumatism, osteoarthritis, depression, etc. The fat medical file that the brigadier wanted me to study in detail held little interest for me. I scanned it quickly; it contained prescriptions; reports of x-rays of the neck, knees and shoulders; blood counts and biochemical parameters; rheumatology and thyroid profiles, etcetera.

I examined Hardayal Singh in some detail. It did not take much time to confirm my initial impression. I wrote out the prescription detailing the dosing instructions and handed it over to the brigadier. I asked him to report back after ten days. He seemed rather dissatisfied and did not ask many questions about the diagnosis or the prognosis for his father. He helped the elderly gentleman out of the chair and the chamber, and left without looking back or saying the customary thank you.

I am generally courteous to my patients and their attendants, whatever their status and situation in life, except when they become overbearing. I thought I had been quite deferential to the man in uniform — I did not understand the reason for his grumpiness.

Brigadier Santokh Sing Mann hailed from Delhi. He had been posted to the brigade in Srinagar a few months earlier. When summer heated up the plains, he had called his father to spend some time with him in Kashmir's salubrious environs. A captain in his brigade had suggested my name when the brigadier had sought a referral for a doctor to see his father. The captain had spoken highly of my clinical acumen and my professional approach. However, our very first encounter had disillusioned the brigadier! He thought that I had been rather casual with the examination — had not even asked for a test to confirm my diagnosis! This must have come as an anticlimax after the hope generated by his junior, especially after his disappointing experience with the doctors who had already seen his father in Delhi.

When he drove to the chemist for the medicines, he sought information from him about me — how was I rated in the medical circles? And what about these drugs I had prescribed for his father and the medical conditions for which they were prescribed? The chemist told him that I was fairly well known in the town, and that the drugs I had prescribed were possibly for a condition called Parkinsonism. The term was new to the brigadier. He wondered why none of the doctors he had earlier consulted had thought of this condition — he even had half-a-mind not to buy the medicines. At home, however, he opened the information folio about the drugs and spent the whole evening reading through them. The long list of side effects enumerated there scared him. Half-heartedly, he administered the first dose to his father and hoped for the best.

In the morning, Hardayal Singh woke up a bit relaxed. That encouraged the brigadier and he decided to go ahead with the medication in the prescribed dose. Within a week, there was a dramatic change. The son could not believe what he saw and what his father reported. The stiffness and pain was all but gone. The face, previously mask-like, wore an expression his son was dying to see again —relaxed and vibrant. The speech had changed from the dull monotone to near vibrancy. The gait had become less stiff and assumed its natural rhythm.

I had asked the brigadier to report back with his father in ten days, but he presented himself alone on the seventh day. As soon as he was shown into my chamber, the burly officer, whose turban almost touched the low ceiling, saluted with a flourish, with a loud click of his boots that shook me out of my chair. He came forward, took my right hand in his large muscular hands, shook it vigorously, and kept shaking it for quite some time.

"I am lost for words," he said, thanking me profusely. "Your medicine has worked like magic! My father is up and about; he is filled with self-confidence at having found himself again after a long time. We cannot believe it."

"I did nothing special," I said in all humility.

"In fact, you did. We had given up hope. The doctors were groping in the dark. During our last meeting, I thought you did not even speak with my father in detail, nor did you look at the tests with much interest or examine him at length."

"On the contrary, I did it all, but you did not realise it. I asked for the information I needed, looked at the tests that I had to, and examined him to my satisfaction. I had diagnosed your father the moment you helped him inside my chamber. It was unmistakable — his stance and gait, his speech, and his appearance. I did not need any more details to confirm my suspicion of Parkinsonism. I did not need to order any tests. In fact, there are none for this condition," I said.

"I can see that in hindsight. Let me confess, I was sceptical about administering the medicines you prescribed." He described his dilemma when he had left my clinic after the first visit. "Thank God, better sense prevailed and I did. But why, if it was so easy to spot the problem did the others miss it?"

"I think it was because, for some reason, he landed with the wrong specialists who don't generally see such patients, though that is no excuse for missing the diagnosis. Every doctor, whatever his specialty, should know about Parkinsonism. I would expect even a medical intern to have made that diagnosis in your father," I said.

"In that case, it seems even more intriguing why it was missed." The brigadier was evidently baffled. "And there were at least four doctors who examined him. You might miss a diagnosis in the first meeting but most of them saw my father several times."

"Well, there can be other reasons. Sometimes—for one reason or another — mostly when they are overwhelmed with work — some doctors do not find the time even to look their patients in the eye, not to speak of noticing how they stand and walk as they enter the consulting chamber. They do not hear their stories in full, which could provide them a deeper insight into the problem. The hospitals are crowded, the outpatient clinics bursting at the seams, and the doctors desperate to finish their quota of patients. I feel that must have been the case with the doctors who treated your father. It is inexcusable, though. Moreover, a doctor needs that extra sense to make the right diagnosis."

"What is the extra sense, doctor?" he asked.

"Intuition," I said.

"How does one get intuition in your profession?" He asked like an inquisitive school boy.

"Well, it is not easy to answer that question. But it comes naturally if one has refined the senses and cultivated the mind."

"I still fail to understand why all the doctors diagnosed

frozen shoulder as the cause of my father's symptoms!" The brigadier would not let go.

"Perhaps the diagnosis was also missed because your father does not have tremors which is a hallmark of Parkinsonism... Besides, your father had the label," I went on.

"Label?"

"Yes, label. I call it the bane of medical practice. A patient gets a label to begin with, which he carries along from one doctor to another like a tag, until someone ignores it and thinks differently, stripping that wrong label off. In the case of your father, the attention of all the doctors went to the stiff shoulders which they labelled as 'frozen shoulders'. Your father has stiff shoulders, no doubt, not because of any joint affliction but from the stiffness of muscles that develops in Parkinsonism. That stiffness also gave him pain in the shoulders and other muscles of the body. That is also why one of them thought he was suffering from rheumatism. In any case, a frozen shoulder is not a diagnosis — it is just a clinical sign. There are so many conditions that lead to frozen shoulders and one has to find the cause in each case. It is like diagnosing a headache as headache and not giving it a definitive label of, say, migraine, or tension headache, or cluster or sinus headache, and so on. Headache is no diagnosis, nor is frozen shoulder."

The brigadier seemed satisfied with the explanation. "Thanks, Doctor. Could I ask a question?"

"Of course."

He had a half-smile, visible in his eyes only, the huge moustache and the groomed beard hiding the other half. "You spent little time listening to the story of my father; and even less in looking into his file ..." It seemed he could still not conceal his initial unhappiness with me.

"Yes, when we listen to the stories, we need to sift fact from fiction and we need to lead the patient to the main story and thwart digressions. More importantly, we need to listen to the patient first, and not let his attendants take over unless he is unable to tell his story for some reason. In the case of your father, he was clear-headed and to the point. I did not need any other details from you except what I asked — certainly, I didn't need an epic narration of how the previous doctors had handled him when it was evident they had missed the diagnosis! Nor did I need to waste a lot of time studying the fat medical folder you wanted me to. I try not to get trapped into a label as I said. I hope you understand."

"I do. Thanks a lot, Doctor."

The brigadier got up, gave me another strong shake of the hand and, in parting, another military salute with a loud click of his boots.

# The Spell

I rang the bell for the next patient.

A familiar face sauntered in, a woman in her early forties, one of my old patients. Ambling beside her was a thin girl, struggling into adolescence.

"*Salaam*, Doctor Sahib." Her tone was familiar, friendly, respectful.

I *salaamed* back.

"Is that your daughter?" I asked, as they took their seats.

"Yes, she is Shabnam, the eldest of my three daughters. You should know her; you have been treating our whole family since the time you pulled me back from the grave. You also rescued her from the clutches of pneumonia nearly eight winters ago. Of course she was small then. She has suddenly leaped out of childhood and grown as tall as a poplar. That is possibly why you did not recognise her."

"Well, that is the way with nature; a tiny seed grows into a big tree."

I had forgotten the woman's name but remembered having diagnosed her as a case of Sheehan's Syndrome several years back when she was brought to me in a semi-comatose state. Since then she had enlisted her whole clan to my patient population.

"How are you doing?" I asked.

"With the grace of Allah, I am fine. I have come for her," she said, pointing to her daughter. "Look how weak she has grown, how pale and frail. She doesn't seem to put on any flesh. While other girls her age are pink and round and robust, she has become like a thin reed. After all, she has come of age; she will have to go to someone's home some day. Who will accept her as a bride in this state of health? What will people think of us? That we don't care; that we do not bring up our children properly..."

"You are quite skinny yourself," I pointed out. "She seems to have inherited your genes."

My patient had been a thin woman ever since I had known her; only lately had she grown a little stouter.

She laughed. "Doctor Sahib, my days are over! At her age, I was plump like a pumpkin, pink like an apple, trotting like a mare. But look at her sallow complexion, wan figure, and the ghostly hollows around her eyes."

"She looks a bit pale, no doubt; but that is probably her complexion," I remarked.

"There is hardly any blood in her system, Doctor Sahib! That is why she has missed her period for two months. I urge her to eat well but she refuses food, does not like her favourite dishes any more and throws up milk. She has lost her appetite. If anything, it is pickles and chutney she wants to live on. She used to be meek and obedient, but of late she has grown moody and cantankerous..."

While the mother was detailing her litany of complaints, the girl kept looking down, fiddling with her nails, avoiding eye contact. She was scantily built, rather hungry-looking, with sharp shiny eyes and a curved mouth, her breasts barely discernible underneath her frock. She looked rather remote and there was no sign of adolescent sensuality. If she was far removed from anything it was womanhood, yet I was on guard. Going by the story her mother narrated, I imagined the first stirrings of life within her.

"Do you have any idea of her age?" I asked.

"Sir, we keep no records of birth, no horoscopes like the Pandits. But I remember she was born during the war."

"Which war are you talking about?"

"Well, the war between India and Pakistan. Remember, when Pakistani women piloted the Sabre jets and waved the green flag as they flew over Kashmir? One of them even dived and plucked a lotus from the Dal Lake as a memento for her countrymen… Shabnam was born during that war."

She was alluding to the Indo-Pak war of 1965 and the fantastic tales that had taken hold of the popular imagination.

I shrugged my shoulders and smiled. It was fairly certain now that her daughter was about sixteen.

"Did Shabnam ever miss her period before?" I asked.

"No, never since they started five years back. There was some irregularity during the first year but she never missed a month. I am sure it is nothing but weakness. Her blood has dried up — how can she have periods? She needs a good tonic, something to restore her appetite and to put some flesh on her bones."

I turned towards the girl to ask a few preliminary questions in order to make her feel at ease. She replied in a low monotone, all the time looking away. She was shy but there was no suggestion of nervousness in her voice. She had never attended a regular school but had received religious education in a *madrasa*. She helped her mother with the household chores and learnt embroidery from her. Her only recreations were hopscotch and jump-rope games with her sisters.

I took my time examining her. She was bony, but there was no evidence of malnutrition, anaemia or jaundice. The examination of her abdomen was normal.

Her symptoms were unmistakable, but if she was pregnant, there were no tell-tale signs… It was still early days.

"I feel I should get a report from a gynaecologist," I addressed the mother after finishing the examination.

She looked at me in utter disbelief. To suggest a gynaecological examination for an unmarried girl was nothing short of blasphemy. It was not done; it had terrible connotations. However, that did not prevent me from suggesting. I knew the lady trusted me implicitly.

"Why, what is wrong with my daughter, Doctor Sahib? What will people think if they see me with her in a gynaecological clinic? It is better to die than be shamed! Why can't you treat her yourself? I am not worried about her periods if that is why you are asking us to see the gynaecologist. They will return once her appetite is restored and her weakness addressed."

I realised it would not be easy to convince her about the need to conduct a pregnancy test on her daughter. The days of ultrasound were still far away. To send her to the laboratory for the test was also fraught with risk. The test had to be carried out in utmost secrecy. Patient confidentiality was not a compelling medical ethic in our part of the world. Rumours travelled faster than wind in these climes. Even if the test were negative, the very fact that pregnancy was suspected would set tongues wagging.

"Let us run a routine urine analysis on her. She may leave

a sample here and we will get it tested. You can see me alone tomorrow; she doesn't need to come." I did not tell her that it was going to be a pregnancy test.

Next evening, when the mother returned, the report confirming pregnancy was on my table. How was I to break the news to her? How would she take it? She might call it outrageous to have sent the urine sample for a pregnancy test without her consent! On the contrary, if she trusted me, how was I to tackle an unwanted pregnancy in an unwed girl? How to ensure that termination was carried out in a sterile and safe environment, preferably in the hospital? Otherwise, she could easily land into the lap of quacks or in the operating dungeons of abortionists with the attendant risks of bleeding and sepsis, even death.

I was battling with these questions even as the mother sat there, trustingly looking at me for a miracle that would bring her daughter back to her perceived idea of good health – plump, with rosy cheeks and a regular menstrual flow. I worried about her other daughters who could land in a similar situation.

I broke the news to her.

"I have to inform you that the urine test has confirmed pregnancy. That is the reason she has had no periods for two months."

"Doctor Sahib, it is not true! It just can't be! I am sure this is some mistake… You saw my daughter yesterday — she is still a tiny little girl! And her abdomen, well, it is flat like the palm of my hand. Do you believe it is holding a life within? How can it be? My girls are pure like the lotus, unsullied by the mud in which it grows, not wet by the water in which it floats. They are incapable of misdeeds; they are far removed from sin, I can assure you. My courtyard is clean. I do not let filth gather, or outsiders pollute it." She was poetic in her distress.

"But it does seem that some outsider has stepped into your courtyard and sown wild oats without your knowledge," I said firmly. "If it is not an outsider, it may very well be one of your trusted people who visit you."

She protested, "I can't believe it. I have always remained vigilant; I do not let any wrong happen to my girls."

"You can't ignore the test result. Rather than protesting, you should be seeking a way out of this unsavoury situation. I am speaking in your interest only. However, you are welcome to seek another opinion."

"No sir, there is no question of going to someone else. You are our family doctor and we trust you fully. I know you will always think and act in our best interest. But I cannot believe my innocent little girl has committed a sin. I will strangle her if she has."

I was quick to dismiss her entrenched notions about

virtue and sin. "Look, it is not my intention to pass judgment. Nor should you. She is so young, so fragile; she doesn't know right from wrong. She has committed no sin. She is a victim of ignorance, an innocent prey of a man's lust. The world is full of predators; she must have been duped. It is the ignorant and the innocent that fall victim to these people. You need to get to the bottom of this. After all, you have other daughters who could be vulnerable."

She was stunned.

After a long silence, she asked, "Meanwhile, what is your advice for Shabnam? Won't you prescribe some medicines to restore her to health?"

I wrote an iron supplement for the girl.

By now, she was fuming with rage, her small eyes flashing in anger, her tiny hands trembling with nervousness. "I will go and dig up the truth and catch the fiend who has heaped ruin on us! My husband will cut off his head!"

As she rose to leave, I cautioned her to exercise restraint with Shabnam and to approach her with compassion to gain her confidence and extract the facts from her.

She returned the next day, bubbling with confidence, a picture of triumph. Fine wrinkles formed on her face as she smiled.

"Doctor Sahib, there has to be a mistake in the test. I have taken my daughter into full confidence. There has been no transgression, no sin. She has sworn by the holy book that she is untouched, unblemished. She is a virgin, pure like the morning dew. I will vouch for my daughters. They are the pride of the neighbourhood. People swear by their virtue. How can iron rust if not exposed to air and water? My daughters do not go anywhere; I do not allow strangers inside my sanctuary. Pregnancy is out of question."

I was astonished by her conviction, her naivety. It was a hard task to drive the brutal truth into her head. "Your daughter *is* pregnant! There has to be a seed sown before a sapling sprouts. I am sure she is hiding something from you. There is a man involved. You have to identify him."

My last words seemed to ring an alarm.

"Talking of a man, yes, Shabnam did tell me of a man chasing her in her dreams. Eerie dreams and nightmares that frighten her so much she cannot recount them fully… But, dreams are after all dreams—unreal, untrue. I often dream of making a pilgrimage — have I made it? Maybe, she needs a pill to give her a restful sleep, undisturbed by nightmares? It may be her state of health that makes her so vulnerable to the fancies of the mind, Doctor Sahib."

"Did you ask her if she can recall the face of the man in her dreams?"

"It is the same dream every time, she told me, and the same man who haunts her, who chases her through a long, narrow tunnel..."

"Where does the chase in the tunnel end? Can she recall

how he looks?"

"Doctor Sahib, my little girl is too frightened to speak. All she can recall is a familiar looking man who approaches her with a sword in his hand. He moves slowly towards her, mesmerising her with his hypnotic gaze. When he gets close, almost to a touching distance, and unsheathes a shining sword, she feels paralysed, unable to move. She can look at him no longer; she shuts her eyes to avoid his gaze. She remembers nothing after that."

"Any likeness to anyone you know?"

"I did ask her, and she said he looks like… our *Pir* Sahib. At the mention of the pir, she started trembling with fear and looked dazed, as if she were dreaming again. She has become moody these days, vacant and withdrawn most of the times."

"Who is this Pir Sahib?" I asked.

"He is our family *pir.*"

"Do you and your daughters visit him often? Does he visit your house?"

"We consult him on all important matters. That is the practice in our community. My girls accompany me sometimes. At other times, he visits us. He is powerful; he has attained special faculties; he has Djinns at his command that can do his bidding."

The mystery was beginning to unravel.

"I do not know, but it is likely he may have commanded

one of his Djinns to frustrate my poor daughter. He may be annoyed with us for some reason."

"In that case, you should avoid him at any cost."

"I avoid inviting him to my house as far as possible since we came to learn that he exercised his spell on some naughty girls in our neighbourhood."

"What did he do?"

Almost whispering in fear, she said: "He has the power to freeze the blood inside their wombs so it stops flowing every month! There was a young girl under his spell. He froze the blood in her womb. Once clotted, no one can unclog the blood and restore the flow, except him."

"Seems to me he is a very nasty person," I exclaimed.

"He is all-powerful. The bigwigs seek him when they have problems. He has a long reach. It is difficult to escape his spell that chases the unfortunate girls even in their dreams."

"Look, I want you to listen carefully. What Shabnam told you is not a dream. Your *pir* is a monster. He needs to be stopped. Otherwise this will continue to happen because the innocent girls will be caught off-guard and fall in the clutches of this vile beast, and credulous mothers like you will be frightened of the consequences of his terrible powers."

She would not believe me. She was so utterly confused and crestfallen—neither able to accept the truth that stared her in the face nor reject the entrenched faith in the powers of the *pir*.

"I feel I must get him to withdraw the spell from my daughter. Meanwhile, I will give her the tonics that you prescribed last time."

I was utterly dismayed as she stood up resolutely from the chair, *salaamed* and left.

ജ്ഞഇ

A week later, she was back in my clinic.

The secretary came in to tell me that she was desperate to see me and would not wait for her turn. "She says it is urgent."

I asked him to send her in.

She was frantic. "Doctor Sahib, you have always rescued me and my family from desperate situations; please don't disappoint me now. Please save the life of my daughter," she said, a little froth forming at the edges of her pinched mouth.

I asked her to take a seat and calm down. "What happened?"

"Shabnam has been bleeding for two days now. I was happy that the spell was finally over, but the bleeding doesn't show any signs of stopping. It is like a tap turned full on. She has fainted several times since the morning."

"I am sorry to hear this. I feel you should move her at once to the hospital. Don't waste time," I urged her. "I will phone the emergency department and join you shortly."

We had to infuse three units of blood and perform curettage to evacuate all the uterine contents. Shabnam was discharged on the request of her mother early the next morning.

A few days later, her mother came to see me. She was carrying a large bag of vegetables. "Thank you for all you did."

"Please take these back; I don't like my patients coming with gifts," I protested.

"I didn't have to buy them. This is home-grown kohlrabi. Shabnam has sent it for you. You can't break a child's heart," she said plaintively.

"I am glad you agreed to bring her to the hospital, otherwise it would have been disastrous. Tell me, what caused Shabnam to bleed?" I asked.

"Did I not tell you, Doctor Sahib? It was the consecrated cup, and the powder," she replied without any affectation.

I was baffled. "Sorry, I didn't understand what you said."

"After I saw you the last time I went straight to Pir Sahib. I fell at his feet and begged him to withdraw the spell and save my daughter. He asked me to fetch a china cup inside which he wrote something in Arabic to undo the spell. He also gave me a powder and asked me to dissolve two spoonfuls in water and feed it to my daughter from the inscribed cup every day for a week. He said it was a herb, sanctified with special invocations. It worked within five days! The clotted blood inside her womb thawed like snow on a sunny day and flowed out like a stream. I am so grateful for his kindness and mercy; thank god, the spell is over."

She *salaamed* and breezed out, leaving me stunned and shaken.

# The Bear Hug

Abdul Razak was admitted to the hospital with symptoms of breathlessness, weakness and fatigue. A salesman with a cloth merchant, he had enjoyed excellent health all 38 years of his life. During the previous week, he started getting breathless while walking and performing routine tasks. Climbing a short flight of stairs made him dizzy and lifting open the shop shutters became an impossible task. He felt tired while attending to his clients.

Abdul Razak was lean and lanky, but with a slightly puffy face. On examination, his blood pressure was low; his pulse fast but so low in volume that it became impalpable during deep breathing. His ankles were slightly swollen, the neck veins stood out, and the liver was enlarged and tender. The heart sounds were feeble and distant, and a faint scratchy sound, the pericardial rub, could be heard in front of the heart near the sternum.

It did not require any special acumen to suspect pericardial effusion— collection of fluid around the heart— as the cause of this clinical presentation.

By the next morning, we had carried out the preliminary investigations, x-rayed his chest, and done an ECG. The heart shadow on the x-ray was large with the classical moneybag appearance, and the ECG findings concurred with the diagnosis of fluid in the pericardium.

What was the cause of pericardial effusion in this patient? His history did not offer any clues. He was not running a fever; there was no history of substance abuse, trauma, rheumatism, allergies or bleeding disorders. All his blood tests, including the hormonal and biochemical profiles were within normal range.

We decided to aspirate the fluid. The year was 1978. Imaging tools other than x-rays were still a far cry. Echocardiography was not available. I tapped the pericardial fluid by introducing a longish needle directed from the abdomen towards the base of the heart—an exercise not entirely devoid of risk even in skilled hands. I watched the syringe fill with bloody fluid. My heart missed a beat! Had I punctured a blood vessel or penetrated the heart? But the blood did not come out in jets and spurts with each heart beat as it would have in that eventuality. Instead, it had to be drawn by gentle suction. Besides, it did not clot. That was a fair indication that the needle was in the pericardial sac and not in the heart. Relaxing somewhat, I drained 130 ml.

Abdul Razak felt relieved of the sensation of pressure on his heart. His breathing quietened down, the pulse volume and blood pressure improved. Microscopic examination of the aspirated fluid also revealed blood. From our experience the main cause of a grossly bloody pericardial effusion was trauma, but on repeated questioning the patient denied any history of injury. Tuberculosis, collagen vascular diseases, bleeding disorders, anticoagulant drugs and cancer could also cause a bloody fluid, but there was nothing to suggest any of these conditions in our patient. Perplexed, we decided to treat him empirically with anti-tubercular regimen, though not without some scepticism. We did this because tubercular pericardial effusion was not an uncommon condition in India, and it was eminently treatable. We did encounter cases now and then with mildly sanguineous effusions in this condition but never one with a grossly bloody effusion.

The patient's sense of relief was short-lived. Overnight, the fluid accumulated again, and the breathing difficulty returned. In the next two days, he developed a typical tamponade—a condition where the fluid in the pericardial sac accumulates quickly in large quantities and hampers the contraction and expansion of the heart, strangulating it, so to speak. Shock and other serious complications could ensue if we did not relieve the tamponade without losing time.

I went in again and drained another 95 ml. Again, it was bloody, and flowed freely into the syringe.

We were baffled. Was this one of those rare haemorrhaging tumours of the heart or pericardium? In that case, would it bleed so fast as to re-accumulate in such a short time? Or was it a bleeding vessel from some other cause? The issue of trauma again surfaced in my mind and I again asked the patient to recall if he was ever hit on the chest or if he had sustained a fall… He could not recall any such event.

In spite of our misgivings, we continued with the anti-tubercular medication. We also put him on high dose steroids in the hope of stabilizing the bleeding, whatever the cause.

We followed up with x-rays from different angles to look for any evidence of a tumour. Nothing! Within three days the fluid re-accumulated and I drained the pericardial sac a third time. By then, he had developed anaemia and we transfused two units of blood, but we were nowhere close to finding the cause of the effusion.

Abdul Razak was a gentle, amiable fellow. He lauded our efforts and even joked about harbouring a spring of the vital fluid in his breast that was gushing out in a fount! He was grateful for the care he was receiving. His attendants were as concerned as we were baffled. I scanned medical literature to refresh my knowledge about the causes of bloody pericardial effusions, and went home brooding over the possible cause in our patient. The more I thought about the case the more I was convinced of it being a case of traumatic effusion, a trauma which he had— somehow—forgotten.

A restless night followed, with a series of frightful dreams. In one, I was drawing buckets of fluid from a well in order to drain it dry, but it kept refilling over and over again. In another, I had been thrown into a ring of bullies who hit me repeatedly on the chest till it swelled and ballooned out like a barrel, jets of blood spouting from numerous holes…

To my surprise, I woke up with a clear mind after such a troubled night. I rushed to the hospital; I was keen to go over Abdul Razak's history again.

The morning rounds started directly with him. He was breathless, and complained of mild chest pain for the first time. The neck veins were bulging again, the liver enlarged, and the heart sounds distant—the unmistakable signs of an overnight re-accumulation.

"Doctor Sahib, when will the blood stop welling up in my heart?" he asked as the team of perplexed doctors stood by his side, trying to grapple with the situation.

"As soon as we determine the cause of your condition," I replied. Then I took a deep breath and asked, with the faintest of hopes, "And now tell me; are you absolutely *certain* you were not hurt?"

Abdul Razak gave me the same confident reply as before. "Yes sir, I am certain I was not hurt."

This was so frustrating!

"Look, I feel that you *have* been hit or crushed by something. Try to recall," I urged him, "did you accidentally slip or fall down? Did anyone slap you in the chest in a joke, or did a cloth roll fall on your chest?"

"I can tell you for certain; nobody hit me, I did not fall, nothing fell on me."

And then I had a flash. "Did someone… hug you… *hard*?"

There was a moment's silence. Abdul Razak closed his eyes and held his head in his cupped hands in deep reflection. And then his eyes widened. "Ah yes, now that you ask! Jamaal, my elder brother returned from the pilgrimage to Mecca. He is the first from our family to have performed the Hajj. We all went to the airport to receive him. It was a great occasion. Though he was gone only for a few weeks, I must have missed him! We rushed into each other's embrace and he hugged me long and hugged me tight. I now recall that I felt a twinge of pain, but forgot about it in the excitement of reunion. I never thought about it since, if that is what you are asking…"

"Exactly, that is what I was looking for, Abdul Razak!" I exclaimed, almost ready to hug him myself.

"What?" he exclaimed, not understanding what I meant.

"A bear hug by a strong man."

"Yes, Jamaal is well-built and strong, but certainly not

a bear," he replied with a child-like smile. "I don't think his hug could have hurt me."

"It tore a blood vessel in the sac of your heart, though!" I could not contain my excitement.

"Jamal is such an angel!" he said with a touch of emotion in his voice.

"We have no reason to believe otherwise," I reassured him. "When did he return from the pilgrimage?"

"A few days before the symptoms started, may be two, or three... However, I was perfectly well in between; I went about my daily routine as before..." He heaved a long sigh and asked earnestly, "I hope he is not the cause of my problem?"

"Your brother did not do it deliberately. You don't have to feel guilty on his score."

"If you really believe it is the bear hug, I hope you won't let him know. He will never forgive himself."

"I do think it was the bear hug. Let me assure you, he will not know unless you want him to."

"He is such a wonderful brother."

"He must be, but his bear hug surely gave us all some sleepless nights," I smiled, and he laughed so loud he became breathless and gripped his chest with his hands.

"Thank you for all you are doing for me," he gasped with great effort.

I addressed my team who had been looking on with

curiosity as the mystery unfolded. "There is no time to lose. Let's call the surgeons before he begins to tamponade again."

The surgeons incised the pericardium and drained the accumulated blood to find the culprit—a bleeding vessel in the pericardial covering. They sutured it and the bleeding stopped. The sac was stitched back. We stopped administering anti-tubercular drugs and steroids.

Abdul Razak improved fast, and he was discharged a week later. Jamaal was there to take him home in a *tonga*. He almost hugged me in gratitude, but I shrank back and offered him my hands instead! He shook them gently and passed his hands gracefully down his flowing beard in a ceremonial gesture.

*Beware of the bear hug*
*Lest it bear down on your tender chest*
*Fracture a rib or tear a vessel*
*Rupture the lung or scratch the heart*

# Malignant Hiccup

Kashi Nath Raina always accompanied his sick wife to my clinic at Karan Nagar. The couple lived alone in a three-storey house right in the centre of a densely populated area around Nai Sarak. A chronic patient of high blood pressure, she was much shorter than him, stocky, and rather grumpy from numerous ailments. She had survived a stroke that left a residual weakness on her left side. She waddled from knee deformities caused by an advanced degree of osteoarthritis. Though I generally avoided making house calls, I did not have the heart to refuse this sprightly old man's persuasions whenever his wife had any major health problem. It was painful for her to navigate the long narrow lane from her home to the nearest means of transport available.

One evening, the couple landed at my clinic. Surprisingly,

it was not his wife but Kashi Nath who occupied the chair meant for patients. I thought it was just an oversight and addressed his wife sitting opposite me, "How are you today, Mrs Raina?"

"I am fine," she said, and looked towards her husband.

Kashi Nath — tall, broad-shouldered and handsome at seventy-five — beamed a smile, but started hiccupping suddenly. Recovering from the bout, he said, almost apologetically, "I am the patient today. She has come to give me moral support."

This was the first time during my long acquaintance with them that he was reporting as a patient. Somehow, I had formed an impression that he was immune from disease, even immortal.

"Well, what ails my healthy young friend?" I asked in a light banter.

He smiled. "I sure feel healthy and young except for what you must have noticed already."

The hiccups returned; he started laughing through them, shy like a child.

"It is my hiccups; they have been bothering me for two days now. They come and go. I feel helpless, embarrassed."

No sooner had he spoken, he started hiccupping again. That made communication difficult and halting. But he went on with his narrative, feeling awkward and apologetic about it. It was disquieting to watch him struggle hard to control the hiccups.

"I have no other problems. There is no pain; my appetite is good, my digestion has never been better. I tried the traditional remedies—ate food without spices and chillies, cut down on my fluid intake, did deep-breathing exercises, consumed antacid gels, even chewed cinnamon and cardamoms—but nothing seems to help. My wife has tried all kinds of tricks to distract my attention from the hiccups, but with little success."

I motioned him to the examination couch. There was nothing remarkable except for the intermittent bouts of hiccups. He had no fever, nor was he jaundiced; his blood pressure, pulse and breathing were normal; his lungs were clear; the heart sounds were perfect. There were no nodes or masses in the neck. His abdomen was soft; there was no tenderness anywhere; no organ enlargement—nothing whatsoever.

There was nothing to go by in this seemingly healthy person.

I was about to prescribe anti-hiccup pills and ask him to report back in a couple of days, hoping it would resolve itself like the transient symptoms that we often encounter in our daily practice which defy understanding. Suddenly, on an intuition, I paused, and asked if he had any explanation for his symptom. Was there anything on his mind, any unsavoury event that might have triggered anxiety?

"Not really," he replied, "but if an emotional upset can cause hiccups, I did have an unpleasant experience just the day before the hiccups began. A young man came to our house to inform us that the gas refills had arrived at the store. He had come to take the empty gas cylinder and the money for the refill. As you know, there is always a shortage of cooking gas — I had been twenty-third on the waiting list for more than a week. I thought this was a godsend. I lost no time in giving him the money and pointing to the empty cylinder in the corner. After he had left with the cylinder on his shoulder, I sensed something wrong, for I realised he was not one of the delivery men I knew. Normally, when the requisition for a refill is admitted, the delivery man brings a filled gas cylinder and takes back the empty one against a proper receipt. This stranger had come without the refill and had taken our empty cylinder and the money without a receipt. As soon as I suspected him to be a cheat, I was at his heels, and gave him chase down the two flights of stairs and out on the lanes, screaming all the while for help. I ran really fast till he was overpowered by the neighbours who had heard my distress calls."

I listened patiently as he spoke through the hiccups.

"He was a swindler, no doubt. You know, it is easier to procure the milk of a sparrow than a gas refill. Thank god, I retrieved the cylinder. But the experience left me drained, physically and emotionally. We were upset and did not sleep well that night, our vulnerability staring us in the face. After all, we are an old couple, living alone and without much help. These are bad times — you can't trust anyone, especially strangers. Nevertheless, we brushed aside the episode as a freak incident and resumed our lives as if nothing had happened. The hiccups started after lunch the next day, nearly eighteen hours after the incident."

"You seem to have run quite some distance, and run really fast." I was imagining the scene.

"Yes, I do not know where I got the energy from — I ran after him like a cop after a thief. Believe me, I felt a boyish thrill when we succeeded in overpowering him! The incident could not have anything to do with these hiccups, could it?"

"Yes, it could," I answered.

"You really think so?"

"I do."

Summing up the sequence of events, here was an old man who had undergone an intensely emotional and physical upheaval — an ideal setting for a heart attack, an acute myocardial infarction. However, the cardinal symptoms and signs were completely missing in this case. He suffered no chest pain or tightness, weakness or giddiness, sweating or indigestion. He was stable in all respects. I had learnt from case reports about myocardial infarction of the inferior wall or base of the heart causing hiccups, although I had never come across a case. Could hiccups be the sole presenting symptom of a heart attack, I asked myself? Yes, they could. My intuition was strengthened by the time interval between the intense exertion and the starting of hiccups, and the fact that there was nothing else to explain the sudden onset of the problem in this old man.

"Mr Raina, I feel you might have sustained a heart attack."

It sounded incredulous to him and he was taken aback for a while, but managed to put up a brave face.

"A heart attack! No, it cannot be. I don't have even a hint of pain. I am fine, fit as a fiddle, except for these hiccups. They are irritating, yes, but not disabling. I am sure they will go away before we know it. And what have hiccups got to do with a heart attack, Doctor Sahib? In fact, if it were not for her," he pointed towards his wife, "I would not even consult you for this problem that all of us experience in our daily lives sometime or other."

"It is good you came. Heart attacks may sometimes occur without any pain, especially in diabetics. Hiccups, although rare in heart attacks, can result from the injured heart muscle irritating the nerve endings in the diaphragm."

He was unconvinced, but his face fell and, for a moment, he looked helplessly towards his wife.

"Mr Raina, it is rather late in the evening and there is no facility for taking an ECG anywhere around here. The nearest place is the hospital. I am going to refer you for admission."

He was shaken by the suggestion. "Doctor Sahib, I do not want to get admitted. We have nobody except ourselves. There is no one to stay with me in the hospital, and no one to take care of my wife? We have not even locked our house properly. Besides, I don't believe I have a heart attack," he pleaded.

"They will run an ECG on you. You need not stay in the hospital if it turns out to be normal," I reassured him.

"Can you please prescribe some medication for now? I will report again in the morning if the hiccups don't stop."

"Complications are known especially in the first few days after a heart attack. I would like you to be in the hospital, under observation," I explained.

"Please, Doctor!" he pleaded like a child.

"I am writing anti-hiccup pills for now. Notwithstanding, I hope you will accept my advice and go directly to the hospital from here. And, please, *don't* walk; hire a *tonga*."

ഈ

The next evening, I found Kashi Nath waiting in my clinic. He was alone and gave me a beguiling smile.

"I am sorry I went straight home yesterday. I hope you understand my situation. It was late and there was no one around to keep my wife company for the night. Thankfully, I feel a lot better with the pills you prescribed. Here is the

ECG. I got it done just now at the Kaul clinic. I hope it does not show a heart attack."

He still hiccupped, but the severity and frequency had abated somewhat. I looked at the ECG. There was unmistakable evidence of a recent heart attack. It was indeed an inferior wall myocardial infarction. I gave him another check-up. There were no new signs. His pulse, blood pressure and breathing were stable. He did not complain of pain.

I came straight to the point.

"Mr Raina, let me explain. The ECG confirms my suspicion. Though this is the fifth day after your heart attack and you are quite stable, and the worst is possibly over, you still need to be in the intensive care unit. Early as well as late complications are known to occur even in minor heart attacks. I advise you to rush straight to the hospital and not lose time.

"If I am stable and the worst is over, why can't I be treated at home, please? I feel quite normal; the hiccups are already on the wane." He seemed convinced about the diagnosis but not about the need to be in the hospital.

"To be on the safe side," I replied.

"How long do I need to be there?"

"Seven to ten days, if all goes well."

"I can hardly afford to leave my ailing wife behind even for a day. However, I will phone my son in the USA; he should be able to fly down at short notice. He could be here within twenty-four hours. After he arrives, I will abide by all you say, even if it means getting admitted for three weeks. For now, please spare me the hospital and treat me at home. I will follow all your instructions faithfully, religiously."

"I suggest you ask some relative or friend to take care of your wife. Meanwhile, I will phone the hospital so they make the arrangements in advance to receive you."

"Before that, I will have to go home, phone my nephew and seek his help." He got up, thanked me, and left.

I shouted after him, "Mr Raina, please go in a *tonga* and don't climb the stairs to your third floor."

"I will do as you say."

Some time later, Chuni Lal Raina, a police officer I knew as a patient, landed in my clinic.

"*Namaskar*, Doctor Sahib. Sorry to bother you; I am here regarding Kashi Nath Raina, your patient. He is my uncle. Does he really need to be in the hospital just for hiccups?" he asked.

"Good to know you are his nephew; I would like you to take charge. Yes, he needs to be under observation for a week or so. He has sustained a heart attack; his hiccup is just a symptom," I explained.

"Hiccups are an everyday occurrence in our daily lives and I thought they are quite harmless. This is the first time I hear they could arise from a heart attack," the nephew said sceptically.

"You are right. Hiccups are common and generally trifling, yet they are not always benign. Persistent hiccups may prove to be the harbinger of a serious underlying condition. Your uncle has sustained a heart attack; we cannot rule out any unforeseen eventuality during the next few days," I replied.

"Thank you for explaining. I will arrange to take him to the hospital." His resolve seemed reassuring.

ഇരുഇരു

The next morning, on getting to the hospital, I rushed to the Intensive Care Unit to check up on Mr Raina. He was not there. I supposed that his nephew had also failed to prevail upon him. The only thing was to hope that he would register an uneventful recovery. I plunged into my hospital routine and tried to put away thoughts about him for the time being.

However, that same evening, just as I parked my car outside my clinic, a funeral procession was passing by. I spotted Chuni Lal in the crowd. He made a sign to tell me he would see me after the cremation. The cremation ground at Chandmari was just a kilometre from my clinic. My heart missed a beat. Could this be Kashi Nath Raina's funeral procession?

A couple of hours later, Chuni Lal announced himself.

"What happened?" I asked.

"Well, I went straight to my uncle after I left your clinic

last evening. I found him in his bed, sitting up, quietly sipping tea and absorbed in a newspaper. He showed no signs of an impending end. In fact, when I saw him sitting there, seemingly unconcerned, I began to wonder if he really had a heart attack. 'You should be all set to move to the hospital rather than taking it easy,' I complained. He smiled his infectious smile and invited me to share a cup of tea with him. That, said he, would give us time to discuss the issue of hospitalisation, for there were many 'loose ends to tie up'. He had contacted his son who was flying the next day to be by his side. 'After Vivek arrives there will be nothing to worry about,' he said with great satisfaction, 'for, as you quite well know, he is a dutiful son and loves us dearly.' Suddenly, he started hiccupping. The cup of tea fell from his hands and he slumped onto the bed. I got up from my chair and moved to resuscitate him but his face had turned deathly white. He was unconscious and breathing fitfully. I put my finger on his pulse; there was none. I put my ear on his breast; there was silence. By then, the breathing had stopped altogether. He was dead!"

A fortnight later, a tall man in his forties landed in my clinic with Kashi Nath Raina's widow. There was no doubt he was the son — so much did he resemble his father. Vivek had flown from the USA to be with his father, but he had arrived too late even for the funeral. Instead of seeing his father alive, he had to perform the ceremonies – ten days of mourning, the immersion of the ashes at Haridwar, and the eleventh and twelfth day ritual ceremonies of oblations to the departed. Now he was taking his mother to Boston and had come to seek my advice regarding her. This was the first time I was seeing her without her husband. She had changed a lot in that short span of two weeks, and looked lost without her husband.

I expressed my sadness on the unfortunate demise. I felt sorry that, in spite of his general good health, he had succumbed.

"If my father was stable all through, what could have caused his sudden death, Doctor?" he asked.

"Cardiac arrest, most likely from an electrical disturbance in the conduction system of the heart. It can occur in two to four percent cases of acute myocardial infarction," I explained.

"Do you think my father could have been saved had he been in the hospital?"

"I can't say with any degree of certitude. Cardiac massage or an electrical shock might have helped restore the heart beat, but not many patients survive after an electrical event like ventricular fibrillation in spite of all we do for them."

"Thank you for having taken care of my parents. I have one question to ask, however. Could you not have persuaded my father a little *harder* to get admitted to the hospital?" He sounded mildly accusatory.

"I tried my very best. I explained the prognosis to your parents, and also to your cousin. Unfortunately, your father shunned the very idea of hospitalisation."

"Could you not have phoned an ambulance to carry him to the hospital? In the USA, doctors in your situation could land in trouble for alleged negligence. You are a highly respected doctor, and I am apt to believe it for you made the correct diagnosis, but that did not save my father."

"It is really sad. Our ambulances are ill-equipped, and the service is erratic. But that was not the issue in this case. The hospital is a stone's throw from here. I could have dropped your father at the hospital in my car had he shown any inclination to accept my advice. But this is Kashmir; our laws are different. We can advise and persuade a patient, not force him against his will."

"I appreciate what you say. Thank you all the same for all you did," he said in a tone of resignation.

I examined his mother, wrote out a prescription for her, and wished her a peaceful stay with her son. But his words that I could have been in trouble rankled. As he got up from his chair to help his mother out, I asked, "Mr Raina, are you the only offspring of your parents?"

"Yes." He looked surprised at this abrupt query.

"How come you left them behind to fend for themselves

in their old age? I have been witness to all that your father had to go through since I have known him, looking after your mother with her numerous afflictions. I do not know about your part of the world but here it would have invited social censure for perceived neglect of one's parents."

He blushed and stood there quite a while, holding his mother by the hand.

"I know what you mean. I often tried to persuade them to accompany me to the USA but I could not have forced them against their wishes." He heaved a deep sigh.

I regretted having given him a taste of his own medicine.

# The Chameleon

Ghulam Mohammad worked in a timber yard at Chattabal in downtown Srinagar. One day, while moving a log on to the saw mill, he lost control and stumbled. The log landed on his head. He was concussed and fell down unconscious. His workmates carried him immediately to SMHS Hospital. By the time they reported in the emergency department, he had recovered consciousness but complained of headache and dizziness. Since we did not have separate neurology or neurosurgical centres in the hospital, the doctors in general surgery took charge of the patient.

The surgeons did not find any evidence of external injury to the scalp. Gross neurological testing showed nothing abnormal, and there was no sign of fracture in the skull x-rays. The patient was given analgesics and kept for overnight observation. By the next morning the headache had subsided and no new signs had appeared. He was discharged and asked to report any new developments.

A week later, Ghulam Mohammad returned to the hospital with a recurrent headache. It was of mild intensity but his wife reported that he had started behaving oddly at times. The doctors found no new signs, so they gave him headache pills, kept him under observation for another night and discharged him the next morning when he reported total relief from the headache.

He was back again in five days. A state of drowsiness and confusion had set in the previous evening. He had staggered while going to the bathroom and was helped to his bed by his wife. When she offered him a cup of tea, he looked at her as if at a stranger, pushed her away, and swore. That was very unusual behaviour from her good-natured husband; she realised something was very wrong with him. Luckily, he went to sleep soon after, and woke up the next morning, fully conscious and cheerful. She heaved a sigh of relief and hoped it had all been a bad dream, but soon after breakfast, he again complained of headache. It was quite severe this time, and he threw up all that he had eaten. That is when he was brought to the hospital a third time.

The doctors found him conscious, communicative and coherent. There was nothing to go by from another detailed examination. Dr Abdul Rashid, the head of the surgical unit, sent his resident to seek my opinion.

By the time I came up to have a look at the patient, Dr Rashid was still making his rounds. He was a jovial person, compassionate to his patients, and a good friend. He was one of those so-called moderate Muslim colleagues who loved to discuss politics with me even though we were on the opposite sides of the political spectrum. He thrived on India-bashing and ridiculing the Indian government for the imposition of its writ on the unwilling Kashmiris, while I debunked the double-speak of Kashmiris, especially the politicians, who milked the Indian secular cow but swore by Islamic Pakistan. He had learnt to be tolerant of differing points of view while on his long stint at Edinburgh for his FRCS. Chatting with him in my spare time was a pleasant change from the busy schedule of teaching, research and clinical work.

Puffing on his cigarette in his characteristic style, Dr Rashid addressed me: "Chowdhury Sahib, you are the lone neurologist around here. This patient has been baffling us with his bizarre symptoms that come and go. We have no idea what is going on. I would love you to join me in my room over a cup of tea after you have examined him."

The year was 1975. Neurology as a sub-specialty was still a decade away in Kashmir. I did not have a postgraduate degree in the subject, nor was I designated as a neurologist, but neurology was my area of interest.

I went over the history again. Ghulam Mohammad's

wife seemed quite intelligent; there was no reason to dismiss her observations about his odd behaviour and fluctuating symptoms. He was a sturdy young man of about thirty, conscious and communicative, but he had no memory of the event leading to the accident and the events that followed, until the time he found himself in the hospital the first time. Nor did he recall the transitory abnormality in his behaviour or the drowsiness which his wife reported. He even laughed with disbelief that he could have misbehaved with his devoted wife, but did not discount it altogether. He thought it was his 'throbbing and tearing' headache that might have put him off. His cognitive functions were normal; he was well orientated to time, place and people.

On a detailed neurological examination, there were no gross signs of any deficit. The motor power in his limbs was good and his perception of pain, temperature and touch were normal, as also his superficial and deep reflexes. However, in spite of a good grip in his right hand, it appeared a bit clumsy and corroborated his wife's observation that it 'did not seem to function as it should.' On a closer examination, I detected a mild impairment of his ability to recognise the size, shape, and texture of objects placed in the right hand. This was a significant finding that pointed to a lesion high on the surface of the left side of the brain where the right hand is represented.

Going by the whole presentation — the history of

trauma, the waxing and waning of symptoms, and the localisation in that area of the brain — I made the diagnosis of subdural haematoma, a collection of blood between the outer two of the three sheaths that envelop the brain.

I walked to Dr Rashid's room to apprise him of my clinical impression and urge him to drain the collection through exploratory burr holes in the skull.

He was forthright as usual. "Chowdhury Sahib, I tend to agree with you, but we have no proof, no way to confirm your diagnosis. He could have subdural haematomas on both the sides. Besides, we have never ventured into this burr-hole business. I sincerely feel that we should refer the patient to the All India Institute of Medical Sciences (AIMS), New Delhi."

I agreed with him. Yes, bilateral haematomas are known to occur in nearly a quarter of the cases. He was a competent surgeon, but he was not the one to venture beyond his familiar territory, or to conduct procedures not attempted by him before, especially when the requisite tools were not available in the hospital. How could I force him to do something which I would not be able to prove before exploration? We had no wherewithal to investigate the patient further in our institution. The age of imaging was still in its infancy. We had heard of CAT scans but not seen one, while MRI and PET scans were not even born. The only way we could confirm our clinical diagnosis would be by performing cerebral angiography for which we did not have the equipment in our institution.

Ghulam Mohammad was referred to AIMS along with a detailed report.

On a Sunday, nearly three weeks later, I was taking a stroll in my lawn when two men led a patient inside, holding him on either side, almost dragging him towards me. I did not like patients barging in on my only off day that I eagerly looked forward to. The patient was laid on the lawn and, before I could vent my annoyance, they disarmed me with an impassioned plea, "We are sorry to have intruded on your Sunday, Doctor Sahib, but this is your case, the one you asked us to take to Delhi."

I had forgotten about the patient but I recognised him immediately.

"What happened? Did you not take him to AIIMS?" I asked.

"We did; we were in Delhi for two weeks. He was examined the day we reported in the Outpatients. The doctor on duty said he was alright and there was no need to admit him since all the beds were occupied. We were asked to show up if his symptoms recurred. We rented a room near the hospital. The patient remained fine. On our next visit a week later, they examined him again, performed an EEG and found nothing wrong. They left it to us to return home or to report after another week. Meanwhile, the headaches went away with the medications they prescribed. We reported a third time. The neurologist gave us a clean chit and we returned home after staying fifteen days in Delhi, feeling rather sore that you had sent us on a wild goose chase, but happy that all was well with our patient. He resumed work in the saw mill soon after and was fine until yesterday when he again complained of headache and developed weakness of the right hand and leg. His speech has become slow and laboured. He drags his leg as you have observed, and cannot hold objects in his right hand. He vomited this morning."

I looked at the case notes from Delhi and found three entries on three different dates, the neurologist having found no abnormal signs each time. However, the evolution of symptoms suggested a rapid and serious development indicative of rising pressure inside the head. I examined the patient where he lay. He was conscious, but slightly disorientated. He suffered from speech disorder, not finding the right words and answers to my questions. His right side was partially paralysed. It was obvious this patient had now accumulated a fairly large collection of blood inside his cranium.

How was I to proceed from here? In the absence of a neurosurgeon in Kashmir, I had to rope in the general surgeons to drill a burr hole in the skull to drain the collection of blood. Prior to it, I had to convince them about the diagnosis, now all the more difficult because the patient had returned from the premier institution of the country with a clean chit!

I asked the patient to report the next morning to my chief resident with a note that the postgraduates examine the case and present him after the rounds.

When the presentation was done the next day, the students came up with the right diagnosis. We decided to perform cerebral angiography. It was a difficult choice since we did not have the necessary equipment; neither had we attempted the procedure before. Nevertheless, we decided to take the bull by the horns and make do with what was available. Dr Shafat Fazili, the radiologist, cooperated fully. He had been my classmate in college and was now a valued colleague who encouraged radiological procedures.

We were lucky. The procedure went off without a glitch. When we looked at the films, there it was—a large subdural haematoma standing out, waiting desperately to be drained. By now the blood collection was pressing on the left side of the brain and pushing it to the right. Delay could mean more complications, even death.

I sent my chief resident to Dr Rashid with the details of the patient. He came down to my room along with his team.

"Dr Chowdhury, I must thank you for going all the way to confirm the diagnosis in this patient. Before we proceed any further, we would like you to explain the angiographic findings. We have never seen a case before and have no idea how an angiogram looks like in subdural haematoma."

I too had not seen one before! I had only read about it in text books and journals, and this was my first attempt. I put up the x-rays in the view-finder and started tracing the course of the main arterial trunks inside the brain and how some of them had been pushed and displaced from the normal course because of the blood collection which showed a cut-off of the vessels.

Dr Rashid blew a long spiral of smoke and addressed his team mates, "There is no doubt about the diagnosis of subdural haematoma. However, as far as I know, none of us here has handled a case before. Is anyone of you prepared to take charge?" He looked quizzically at his assistant professor, Dr Abdul Ahad Guroo, a dynamic young surgeon always ready to have a go at difficult cases, always ready to try new things.

Dr Guroo at once volunteered. "I will give it a try. It would be wonderful to have Dr Chowdhury with us in the theatre."

That was a clear call for moral support. It is surprising how physicians hardly ever follow their cases into the operation theatre once they have diagnosed and handed them over to the surgeons. I must have sent them scores of acute appendicitis, gallstones and duodenal ulcers, but hardly ever watched an appendix or a gall bladder being surgically removed. In the present case, I readily agreed to join the surgical team.

The patient's head was shaved and he was taken to the theatre. We outlined the area on the scalp to be explored. Dr Guroo made a small incision, reflected a flap of the scalp, exposed the bone and drilled a large hole till the outermost covering, the duramater, was visible. He punctured the duramater. Dark blood started flowing out. Nearly 200 ml was drained. The hole was sealed with the scalp flap. To everyone's relief, it turned out to be a clean operation.

Ghulam Mohammad recovered fast. By next morning he was free of headache. The power of his limbs returned in a few days. He walked unaided on the sixth day and was discharged on the eighth. He resumed work after three weeks.

# The Boy Who Wanted to Grow Tall

On a warm summer evening of the year 1979, Bushan Lal strode into my clinic, a short, squat boy in tow. He was a close relative and confidant.

"This is Ashu, my sister's son," he said, introducing the boy. "His mother has been urging me to accompany him here for some time now. There is no problem except that he seems rather short for his years. 'Who will marry him when he comes of age if he doesn't gain height?' she moans whenever I visit her."

I chuckled. "Is that her main concern, marriage?"

"There are other concerns too. Ashu has become rather pensive. He broods a lot about his stature. It has started affecting his grades at school...Could you prescribe supplements that may help him gain a few inches?" He spoke matter-of-factly, seemingly from the belief that there were potions for the asking that would help a person grow tall.

The boy looked at me eagerly.

"There are no supplements I know of that increase height," I replied.

"But there must be a way out. I read somewhere in a magazine about hormones that stimulate height." He was certainly well-informed.

"Growth hormone is available for hormone-deficient kids. If administered before puberty, it may help them gain height. However, such cases are rare. One has to be sure about the diagnosis since the drug is costly and has to be given in the form of injections over a long period of time. In any case, we have to find out what we are dealing with in this boy," I explained.

"We don't mind the cost and the duration of treatment as long as it helps. He is the shortest amongst his classmates and the butt of their ridicule. That is why he is so desperate to gain a few inches."

I directed my attention to the boy. He avoided my gaze, looking away at the painting on the wall. Shy, short and stout, he had a thick crop of hair on his round head. He was certainly dwarfish.

"What is your age, Ashu?" I asked.

"I will be fifteen in two months." His voice had not broken yet, and he sounded rather feminine for a thickset boy. On inquiry, he did not complain of anything referable to any organ or system. He ate with relish, slept well, had no visual problems and suffered no headaches.

"Why are you so impatient? There is still time for you to grow. Some kids grow slower than others," I tried to reassure him, even as I suspected the diagnosis of Frohlich's Syndrome.

"But he has not gained any height now for a whole year! His sibling, three years younger, has already caught up with him. Well-meaning relatives ask him if he has grown any taller and the not-so-well-meaning classmates tease him that he never will; friends commiserate with him, and strangers snigger at him, while teachers inadvertently blurt out 'you midget' when they are annoyed with him. His mother constantly bemoans her fate because her son is too short. It seems the whole world is preoccupied with his height; no wonder he is fixated on it too. He measures himself obsessively, follows diets that claim to boost height, cycles up the steep roads, jumps ropes and hangs from crossbars, but nothing seems to work. He has grown depressed and irritable. You will have to do something."

I happened to know the parents of the boy. His mother was of medium stature, but his father was certainly taller than an average Kashmiri male. Since his younger brother was already taller than him, a genetic factor for dwarfism seemed unlikely. The only striking features were his voice and the paucity of secondary sexual characters – his penis was partly buried in thick pubic fat and the testes were small.

In a nutshell, here was a healthy looking fifteen-year-old boy with subtle signs pointing to the pituitary-hypothalamic axis in the brain – growth failure, delayed puberty, and adiposity – that reinforced my initial impression.

I ordered an x-ray of his skull. Bushan Lal looked at me with an expression of incredulity. All he had come for was a nutritional supplement or a growth stimulant for the boy; he had not bargained for any detailed examination or investigations!

"We need the x-ray to rule out any treatable condition in the brain," I said, careful not to mention the word tumour or cyst. That was to obviate any discussion at this stage.

"You may bring the x-ray tomorrow; Ashu does not need to come."

Bushan Lal was back the next day, the boy in tow. He placed the x-ray on my table, and there it was – the classical eggshell calcification in the pituitary area right in the middle of the skull, unmistakable of a large tumour, a craniopharyngioma.

"I had asked you not to bring Ashu along."

"He wanted to come. He lost sleep wondering if he really had something wrong inside his head. He is quite mature for his age and you may feel free to speak with both of us," Bushan Lal assured me.

"Ashu has a craniopharyngioma in his brain. It is a cystic tumour of the pituitary gland that has grown over the years and he may need surgery to excise it."

Bushan Lal stared at me in disbelief. Was I sure of the diagnosis? Could it be something else, something simpler? What had a cyst to do with his height? Could we not let it be? Who would conduct the surgery? Was it difficult, hazardous? If surgery was performed, would that gain him the height? Was it binding to do it now or could he wait?

These and many other questions were fired at me one after the other. Pertinent questions, no doubt!

I told them that I was fairly confident of my clinical impression. I would refer him to AIIMS, Delhi. If we left the cyst alone, it might expand, compress and damage various structures that came in its way, with serious consequences – visual deficits, raised pressure in the brain, headaches, convulsions, endocrine and autonomic damage, etc. By removing as much of the cyst as possible, we could arrest the symptoms and prevent further damage. As to height, well, he might gain it, but there was no guarantee. Yes, surgery was difficult and there could be complications because of the location of the cyst at the most critical junction between the brain, the visual pathways and the endocrine system. I placed all the cards on the table.

There was grim silence in the room. Bushan Lal started tapping his foot anxiously on the floor. He looked at the boy inquiringly.

Ashu's stance suddenly changed; he seemed to stand taller. He looked at me, his eyes fiery, his face strangely animated. His hurried, high pitched voice broke the silence that had descended on the room. "I am willing to get the tumor removed. I want to be tall. Please can I have the surgery?"

"Give it a serious thought. You will have to discuss it with your parents," I told him.

Bushan Lal returned the next day to collect my referral letter to AIIMS. It seems that a family drama had ensued after Ashu proclaimed that he was ready for surgery. His father expressed reservations about it, but Ashu was so charged that he accused him of not wanting to do enough. He dismissed every concern about the possible risks. 'I would rather die on the operation table than suffer the shame of being mocked as a dwarf for the rest of my life,' he stood adamant.

The 'midget' was raring to set sail on the voyage to Delhi, and return tall.

ຍ໙ຍ໙

In my busy schedule I had all but forgotten about the boy when I got a distress call from Delhi. It was Bushan Lal. "Ashu is battling for his life. Can you please phone the neurosurgeon?" he pleaded.

I phoned the surgeon. It had been a difficult surgery. The tumour was quite large and almost embedded in the hypothalamus. They had been very careful dissecting it from its bed, but there must have been significant injury to the hypothalamus. The boy had developed a rapid heart-beat, high blood pressure, excessive sweating and high temperature— signs of an Autonomic Storm. It was a desperate situation. They had failed to control the high temperature, to maintain hydration, to keep the blood pressure under check with all the available drugs. Ashu was in coma; the situation looked grim.

Bushan Lal came to see me a week later. He seemed to have aged.

"I feel responsible for Ashu's death. He was in excellent health and breezing through life; his height more of a psychological handicap than a physical disability. For all I know, he would still have been frolicking around, living many useful years. I keep thinking about the evening before we embarked for Delhi. Ashu couldn't contain his joy; in fact, he was ecstatic. He was so excited he had lost sleep adding inches to his height. He told me he was going to be the tallest kid in his class. I can still hear him laughing and whistling in secret joy. Little did I know that I was taking him on his last journey."

I had no words to console him. I myself felt numbed at the loss of a young life. But that is a cross doctors have to bear sometimes even as they try to proffer what they believe is the best advice. Ashu might have lived some more years without any major symptoms, but the tumour would have ultimately caught up with him to cause crippling neurological complications. After all these years, I still feel a twinge of pain in my heart when I think of him. Alas, the boy who wanted to grow tall at any cost never lived to realise his dream.

# A Timely Incision

The 1960s and 70s were breakthrough years in the expansion of medical facilities in Jammu and Kashmir. Medical College Srinagar, the first medical institution in the state, produced its first graduates in 1964. Post-graduate courses began on a small scale in the following years. Massive recruitments in the teaching faculty followed and generated an exciting academic and research atmosphere. The introduction of modern investigative tools and the holding of academic seminars and journal clubs helped in refining teaching methods and improving patient care. By the early 80s, the college was a bustling campus, and a favoured destination for national and international medical conferences.

However, subspecialties remained undeveloped for a long time. We had started an intensive coronary care unit, but not a full-fledged department of cardiology. A colleague started endoscopies as a modest step towards establishing gastroenterology. Neurology was represented by the Tuesday Clinics that were held in my chamber, and the neurological investigations—myelography, air encephalography and carotid angiography—were started in collaboration with the radiologists. There were no equivalent surgical subspecialties like neurosurgery, or cardiovascular and thoracic surgery. Difficult cases pertaining to these disciplines landed in the PGI, Chandigarh, or the AIIMS, New Delhi. That meant a lot of inconvenience and expense for the patients.

Nevertheless, we tried to handle emergencies in these disciplines with whatever facilities were available. In the process, we were experimenting, innovating, and learning. Some of us wanted to give our best, waiting for a chance to translate our visions into reality, and to move from the mundane to the cutting edge. That is how institutions grow—by the industry and application of the people who man them.

I was the de-facto neurologist in the institution because of my special aptitude and interest in the subject and not because of any higher academic qualifications. I always believed that clinical diagnosis was the bedrock of the practice of medicine and that one's interest and diligence were the best qualifications. I often received neurological referrals from my colleagues.

One such case was referred to me by an orthopaedic surgeon in 1979. Akram was a 45-year-old male who had developed sudden, severe pain in his right leg. Five hours later, an orthopaedic surgeon admitted him in the hospital with the diagnosis of acute lumbar disc prolapse. He ordered x-rays of the spine, and put the patient on pain killers, bed rest and traction—that was the treatment in vogue. Instead of getting any relief, Akram started crying with pain and was unable to move his leg. The next morning, the surgeon examined him again. He believed that the disc prolapse was causing severe compression of the nerves emerging from the spinal cord and producing a significant weakness of the leg that mandated immediate surgical intervention and removal of the disc. He sought my opinion.

I went over the history again. Akram had started with sudden searing pain in the leg the previous morning. The pain did not refer to any particular distribution of nerves on the leg, but the whole of it down the thigh. It got worse when he attempted to move his leg, but not when he coughed or moved his spine. He had no history of having strained his back or lifting a heavy object—the two common events that cause acute lumbar disc prolapse. Soon after traction, he had felt numbness and weakness in the right leg, and noticed that his foot was turning bluish. He was in great distress.

On examination, I noticed a purple flush over his nose and cheeks. The pulse was fast, thin, and grossly irregular.

Blood pressure was low.

The right leg was cold, the right foot pale, the toes were blue, and the sole blanched on pressure. In the groin, the femoral artery — the vessel that supplies blood to the leg — was distinctly palpable and bounding, but when I traced it down nearly an inch, it became very tender. Beyond that tender spot, all pulsations in the leg were absent. I could not feel the pulse behind the knee, nor around the ankle or foot. There was motor weakness of the right leg below the knee, but the sensations were intact and the tendon jerks normal. The left leg was normal in all respects; so was the spine.

In view of the absence of pulse in the left leg and the total clinical presentation, this was a straightforward case of femoral artery block, most likely from an embolus. The source of the embolus was not far to seek. On auscultation of the heart, I heard the classical diastolic rumble of mitral stenosis — a narrowing of the mitral valve. The irregularly irregular pulse pointed to auricular fibrillation that we confirmed on the ECG. The chest x-ray was characteristic of mitral valve stenosis and left us in no doubt about the source of the embolus being the left auricle of the heart.

This was not a neurological but a vascular emergency. The cardiac status was not compromised and it did not need any active intervention at present except to administer drugs to reduce the heart rate. But to salvage the leg, we had to re-establish the blood flow. This called for removal of the embolus lodged in the femoral artery. Delay could cause gangrene of the foot and lead to several complications — infection, septicaemia, and the need for amputation.

Akram was a barber of modest means. Time was running out. It was out of the question to refer him to a cardiovascular unit at Chandigarh or Delhi. We had to act fast.

Who amongst my surgical colleagues was most likely to rise to the occasion and perform the embolectomy, a procedure never attempted before in our institution? Dr Sheetal Singh came to my mind. Here was the opportunity he was waiting for. He was a general surgeon, fresh from the UK with an FRCS. Flamboyant, friendly, and full of enthusiasm, he was a new appointee to the Medical College faculty and had established a good reputation as one who dared to take chances and tread where other surgeons feared to go.

I called him. He was with me in a flash.

"Sheetal, I have a case for you. This young man is afflicted with a rheumatic heart. He has a mitral stenosis and is fibrillating. He has thrown a large embolus which is blocking his right femoral. It calls for an urgent intervention otherwise gangrene might set in," I said summing it up.

"But this is vascular surgery! I have hardly ever watched, let alone assisted in cardiac or vascular surgery! In any case, don't you think we need to perform an angiography to localise the embolus before we venture to perform an embolectomy?" He sounded apprehensive but not totally reluctant. He was right, but we had no access to imaging techniques like the Doppler ultrasound, conventional angiography or digital subtraction angiography, which provide an accurate picture of the blood vessels.

"You do not need an angiography in this case. You can feel the embolus right here under your finger." I pointed to the groin of the patient and marked a circle on the skin over the blocked site with my pen.

"All you have to do is to incise the artery lengthwise at this site, remove the embolus and stitch it back." I made it sound very simple. "The actual procedure should not take more than a few minutes. I would love to watch how you go about it and make history."

If there was any hesitation, it was gone. Suddenly, he was enthused, raring to go.

We lost no time. The patient was wheeled into the theatre; I joined the surgical team.

While going through the preliminaries of washing up, Dr Sheetal Singh kept talking, relating interesting anecdotes from his stay in the UK. I felt it was to diffuse the tension that might have built up inside him. The anaesthetist injected local anaesthesia at the site of surgery. When time came for the incision he looked at me.

"Let us expose the femoral artery." I said.

He made a clean incision. With a little dissection, he

exposed the artery.

"The artery is quite superficial here. Let us palpate it and trace it down to see where the pulsations stop." He knew the steps; I was speaking more to engage him in conversation and take the pressure off him.

He spotted the site of the blocked segment of the artery and his voice boomed with excitement, "The embolus is lodged right here; I can feel it under my finger tip."

"Bravo!" I said appreciatively.

He clamped the artery above the blocked site. Deftly, he made a small incision the size of a small buttonhole in the artery. He retracted the incised segment; the clot came into view. He eased it out gently through the nick. It was a large, dark-red, sausage-shaped embolus, nearly an inch long and quarter inch in width. The incised artery was sutured and the clamp released. There was no bleeding, whatsoever; just a little oozing. The skin was stitched back. The circulation in the leg was immediately restored, and the colour returned to the leg in no time.

There was jubilation in the theatre! This was history being made – the first case of embolectomy in our institution.

"Congratulations, you have done it!"

"I did not realise it would be so easy."

"It became easy the moment you accepted the challenge. All it took was nick and someone willing to make it."

# To Nudge a Brain

Romesh was brought to our intensive care unit in an unconscious state. He had survived cardiac arrest at home.

This young man of thirty-three had been fine until a day earlier when he had come down with acute diarrhoea and vomiting. A chemist gave him metronidazole, chlorpromazine and an anti-diarrhoea mixture. At around ten in the morning, he had developed palpitations, sweating, weakness, and dizziness. His brother found him deathly pale, and could not feel his pulse. He rushed him to the hospital.

When we examined Romesh, he was in a deep coma, but the pulse had returned. It was fast and feeble. The blood pressure was low; the respirations were deep with pauses, and the temperature 96 F. He was lying limp and flaccid, without any spontaneous movement, unresponsive to verbal commands and to external stimuli. The pupils were semi-dilated, and non-reactive to light. All the superficial reflexes and tendon jerks were absent.

We started an intravenous line to administer fluids and drugs, and introduced an in-dwelling catheter into his bladder. The blood pressure and pulse normalised within the next three hours; urinary output remained satisfactory, and the other vital signs improved rapidly. But he continued to remain in coma over the following days.

On the fifth day of admission, the intravenous line was withdrawn and tube feeding started. A long vigil for the return of his consciousness ensued thereafter. It continued for several weeks. We graded the coma every day to monitor the condition. There was not a flicker of spontaneous movement anywhere. He continued to remain in grade four coma—unresponsive to sound, touch, pressure, pinprick, stroking of the soles, or gentle shaking of the body. His pupils remained unchanged and non- reacting to light. All the reflexes remained absent. We would have liked to find the presence of electrical activity in his brain but back in 1975 we didn't have an EEG machine.

Romesh belonged to a family of Punjabis who came to Kashmir during the Dogra rule, and settled down predominantly in the Maharaj Gunj and Harising High Street localities. They were a well-knit clan of businessmen who traded in spices, tea, edible oil, and other food items imported from the plains to the valley. Romesh's family members took turns to watch over him and help in his nursing. It involved removing secretions from his mouth, tube-feeding, turning sides, cleaning, washing, and changing bed linen. In spite of their meticulous care, he developed multiple bedsores, some of them almost baring the bone underneath. His attendants stuck to their jobs with unrelenting dedication and quickly learnt the knack of dressing the sores. They did not show any signs of weariness even as we were feeling hopeless about the state of the patient, and considered him brain-dead for all intents and purposes. We would have liked to discharge him in that condition but for their keen desire to keep him under our watch. We examined him every day and ensured proper hydration and nutrition. It was surprising that even as we debated the situation amongst ourselves and believed that the patient was in a permanent vegetative state from which there was no possibility of recovery to normal cognition, the family showed no signs of giving up.

Weeks passed. Some of the sores started healing, but his coma was unrelenting. Suraj, the elder brother of the patient, ventured to ask one day as he followed me out of the intensive care after we had finished the morning round, "Sir, how long will it take for him to open his eyes and speak?"

I was prepared for that question but that did not make it any easier to pronounce the grim verdict. "It seems Romesh has entered a vegetative state from which he is unlikely to come out."

"How can that be? He is so young and strong; he would climb the Shankaracharya hill faster than any of us, play cricket like a champion, open the bowling for our team, and hurl the ball like a meteor. Each one of us comes down with an attack of diarrhoea some time or other... how often does it send a healthy man into a vegetative state?"

"Hardly ever, but your brother has sustained severe brain damage due to cardiac arrest which must have lasted more than five or six minutes. His brain does not respond to any stimuli; it has shut down completely. The chances of recovery get dimmer with every passing day," I tried to explain in layman's terms.

"Why did he develop cardiac arrest, Doctor Sahib?"

"We are trying to figure that out," I answered without going into the details that he was unlikely to understand. We had found the cause, though – a condition called 'Torsades de pointes', a rare disorder of heart rhythm resulting in episodes of very rapid heart rate and, sometimes, cardiac arrest. The clue lay in his ECG.

"He seems to be in a deep sleep from where he may yet wake up. Isn't there anything that might *nudge* his brain back into activity?" Suraj asked with a teenager's inquisitiveness.

"I really don't know. There is very little we can do in such a situation except to provide life-support and hope for the best." It was an acknowledgement of our ignorance about the large grey areas at the frontiers of neurosciences waiting for exploration. It was also a philosophical resignation to the unknown forces that determine the outcome in a patient after the medical professionals have exhausted all their skills.

Cricket season was in full swing. The first test match between India and Pakistan had started. People were glued to their transistor radios. Offices, homes, shops and stores buzzed with the ball-by-ball running commentary, the familiar cadence of which absorbed the lives of almost everyone, young and old alike. The next five days would be one of swaying emotions, of elation and depression, depending on the see-sawing fortunes of the teams. Television had not yet arrived in Kashmir — people went about their business carrying transistor radios, holding them close to their ears so as not to miss anything.

During our morning rounds in the intensive care unit, we found Suraj sitting by the side of his unconscious brother holding a transistor radio to his ear. The cricket commentary was on.

I was amused at this sight. "What are you trying to do?" I asked.

"Cricket is the passion of my brother's life. There is nothing that would excite him more. He has never ever missed the running commentary of any match that India played. I feel I ought to keep it on for him, just in case he is listening. His idol, Sunil Gavaskar, has opened the Indian innings and is going great guns."

I was moved by his commitment to his brother and his unflinching optimism. Gavaskar, the cricketing legend, had already scored sixty runs. There was a crescendo of roars from the crowd at every shot he played as the commentators raised the pitch with every ball he sent to the ropes. Suraj was greatly animated and held the transistor even closer to his brother's ear.

I did not have the heart to tell him that this was an exercise in futility, that it was a vain hope that the patient could hear the commentary in his comatose state.

On our rounds the next day, we again found Suraj holding the radio to his brother's ear. When he saw us approaching, he rose from the chair, and rushed towards us, beaming with excitement. "Doctor Sahib, you have to see this!"

There was a triumphant note in his voice. He switched on the radio, held it near his brother's ear, and turned the volume knob to high. As the commentary boomed, the patient's eyelids flickered. Suraj turned off the radio; the flickering stopped. He turned it on again; the flickering returned.

It was amazing. We tried to find out if Romesh would respond to verbal commands. We shouted his name in his ear; there was no response. We tried other questions, shaking him lightly for a response; there was none. We again turned on the radio and tuned it to a music channel; it had no effect. We tuned it again to the running commentary; his eyelids flickered one more time. We switched it off and tried other stimuli. We stroked the patient's soles and pinched his skin; it did not make any impression.

There was no going back from there. Suraj, and the other attendants, held the radio near the patient's ear without letting up. Each time there was the excitement of a four being hit, or a catch dropped, or a batsman given out, Romesh responded with a flickering of his eyelids, and sometimes, a momentary opening of his eyes. On the fourth day of the match, his eyes opened wider and he looked around vacantly as if woken from a long dream whenever the commentary was on. By the fifth day, the match ended and so did our despair. We were all enthused by the unmistakable signs of recovery of his mental functions as he started responding to other stimuli and to our commands. He also made attempts at spontaneous movements of his head, neck and limbs and struggled to get out of bed. Over the next week, the improvement was dramatic. He raised his limbs in response to commands; he made eye contact and started mumbling words; he grasped our hands in a gesture of affection.

It was during the third week after he was exposed to the cricket commentary that Romesh started recognizing his mother and siblings and called them by their names, speaking the first clear words. The bedsore healed rapidly as we made him sit up and helped him walk. Fourteen weeks after admission, when we sent him back home, he was walking unaided, feeding himself, speaking almost normally, and restored to full cognition.

Romesh returned to normal life a month after discharge. Another month passed and he was back in the cricket arena, playing his favourite game. He and his family taught us never to give up hope, never to lose faith, and to *nudge* our imagination just like the favourite cricket commentary nudged his *hibernating* brain.

*The human body, what a marvel*
*How amazing it's potential!*
*Bones broken into shards*
*Unite to become whole again;*
*Ruptured muscles mend,*
*Torn ligaments reconnect;*
*Gashes heal, wounds fill up;*
*Nerves re-grow and regenerate;*
*Brains hibernate, to wake up again.*

## Blazing a Diagnostic Trail

I had taken up a one-year assignment as a physician at Bimaristane Akhwan in the city of Kashan. Those were relatively peaceful times in Iran under the rule of the Shah who was overthrown by the revolution soon after I left the country. Kashan is about 200 km from Tehran, the capital of Iran. It is famous for carpets. The people are mostly carpet weavers and traders. They are, nearly all, Shia Muslims — cultured and outgoing.

Being the lone internist in the hospital, I ran both the outpatient as well as the inpatient service. Dr Ghaznavi, the hospital administrator, helped me with the outpatients during the morning shift. He was the leading medical practitioner of the town and we got along well.

One day, we were almost done with the morning rush of

patients. Dr Ghaznavi had taken off his apron and washed his hands when a patient was brought in on a stretcher. Still drying his hands on a towel, he looked at the patient and called the nurse.

"Miss Nayeemi, look this woman is here again. We don't have the wherewithal to deal with a case of paraplegia in our hospital! Could you please direct her attendants to take her to Tehran." After wishing me good day, he left, without examining the patient.

The word paraplegia rang a personal note in my ears. I had written a thesis on the subject way back in 1966 while pursuing my postgraduate degree. It was a hard-earned degree that shaped my career as a physician, and got me interested in neurology. I would not easily let go of this patient without examining her. I asked Miss Nayeemi to hold back the patient for a while so I could look her over after finishing with my patients.

Later, I approached the woman on the stretcher. Her appearance was striking – a pale and puffy face with fine wrinkles that made her look older than her thirty-three years. She was too lethargic, hazy and weak to relate her story. She did not even attempt to move her limbs or turn onto her sides. Her voice was croaky, her skin rough and cold. It did not need any special acumen to diagnose Myxoedema, a condition resulting from hypo-function of the thyroid gland.

The attendants stated that she had become progressively

dull, slow, sluggish, and enfeebled over the last decade. Gradually, she had lost interest in the daily chores which she took longer to perform, finally stopping altogether. Her appetite had decreased; she felt unusually cold even in summer, and was generally constipated. During the previous year, she had become too weak to walk and lay in bed most of the time, her limbs stiff and flexed at the knees and elbows. It was because of her inability to walk that Dr Ghaznavi had labelled her as a paraplegic.

The obstetric history was revealing. She had given birth to three children, each after a normal delivery. Her menstrual period had not resumed after the last delivery ten years earlier during which she had bled excessively. There had been failure of lactation and the new-born was fed formula milk. Over the years, she had lost her libido, and her husband had given her up as stupid and hopeless and taken another wife.

Examination revealed a low pulse rate, low blood pressure, subnormal temperature and slow, shallow breathing. She was conscious, but her responses were scanty and slow. The breasts were atrophied, the skin coarse, the limbs stiff, the tendon reflexes characteristically delayed. There was no evidence of paralysis of legs, or paraplegia.

I admitted the patient.

ഇരുഇരു

It was a feeling of deja vu. I went down memory lane to

a similar case I had diagnosed a decade earlier, back home in Srinagar. That day, I was in my office chamber for a snack and coffee after the morning rounds, when a person claiming to be my old neighbour from Rajveri Kadal, was let in by the orderly.

"Doctor Sahib, my wife is dying. She is barely thirty-five. I have taken her to several doctors but her illness has remained an enigma. She is in a terminal state and I have even procured a shroud and made arrangements for her funeral, just in case. You must come and see her."

He seemed desperate. I was not happy visiting a dying person who had been given up as hopeless, but I felt I had no choice.

The house was a block away from Rajveri Kadal, where I was born and brought up until I left Kashmir for medical studies. The patient had been laid on a mattress on the floor. A few flies buzzed around and sat on the muslin gauze that covered her face. I removed the gauze to behold a pathetic looking woman, drowsy, responding only to painful stimuli, unable to communicate and barely able to swallow water. Her looks were striking, like the patient in Kashan — coarse, pale and puffy. Her skin was cold and rough, her pulse slow and shallow, and the blood pressure low. The hair on her head was coarse and scanty. Her trousers smelt of urine from lack of bladder control.

A battery of tests had been conducted during her past

examinations, including chest and skull x-rays. These were within the normal range.

I suspected—nay, I was almost certain—that this was a case of severe hypothyroidism going into pre-coma. I introduced a feeding tube down into her stomach, and an in-dwelling catheter into her bladder, and explained about care-giving, feeding, and medication. I started her on thyroxin.

The recovery had been so rapid and striking that she walked to my clinic in four weeks! It was then that I reviewed the full obstetric history, which was almost similar to the Kashan case, strongly suggesting the diagnosis of Sheehan's Syndrome, and not just simple hypothyroidism. That explained her failure to menstruate and lactate after her last delivery and the low blood pressure. I added replacement therapy for the adrenal and gonadal hypo-function.

The transformation was amazing. She looked younger and prettier by the day. And I became a celebrity in my old neighbourhood. A spate of cases followed after I presented the patient in the fortnightly seminars at the Srinagar Medical College where I was a faculty.

That was in 1969. Now, nine years later, I was face to face with an exact replica of the case I had seen back home. Like Kashmir, special lab facilities, especially the hormonal assays, were unavailable in Kashan.

I started the patient on replacement therapy – thyroxin, prednisone, and estrogens – and left for my lodgings, but not before I phoned Dr Ghaznavi to inform him that I had admitted his case of 'paraplegia', and would like him to examine her and let me know his clinical impressions.

Late in the evening, Dr Ghaznavi phoned back to tell me that he had examined the patient but not been able to make head or tail. Would I please let him know what I thought?

I asked him to read about the diseases of the pituitary so we could discuss the case the next morning.

A senior physician and a busy practitioner of Kashan, Dr Ghaznavi was one of those rare specimens in the medical fraternity who did not feel offended if a misdiagnosis was pointed out. On the contrary, he was ready to learn about new disease entities and syndromes, and new techniques. He had opened the textbook of medicine and gone through the chapters on the diseases of pituitary. He had carried the textbook with him to the hospital early next morning and examined the patient once again.

When I arrived, I saw a beaming Dr Ghaznavi waiting for me at the top of the long flight of stairs leading to the hospital building. He shook my hands repeatedly and hugged me right and left in the Iranian style, finally landing a kiss on my cheek.

"*Khaeli mamnoon* – very grateful, Dr Chowdhury."

"You sound ecstatic this morning!" I remarked.

"I am. I hope I am not wrong this time about the patient. I feel she is a textbook picture of Sheehan's Syndrome — unless you fault me again."

"You are spot on."

"You have blazed a new trail of diagnosis for us in Kashan. I now realise, we may have in this city many more cases of undiagnosed Sheehan's syndrome."

The patient who was brought on a stretcher went away walking after three weeks. Dr Ghaznavi spread the word and it was not long before other physicians practicing in Kashan and the neighbouring villages started pouring in during my evening shifts with their problem cases. The awareness of Sheehan's Syndrome brought out a flurry of undiagnosed cases. Within the next ten weeks, we dealt with sixteen cases. A seminar was held on the subject, initiating an academic atmosphere in the town.

It turned out that giving birth to several children was common in Iran — the average woman conceived every two to three years and went on producing children as long as she was fertile. Family planning was an alien concept. It was not unusual for couples to have enough children to assemble a football team on their own! Complications were common because deliveries were often conducted at home by midwives. Nobody had heard of Sheehan's Syndrome. What the mind did not know, the eyes failed to see.

The cases, both in Kashmir and Kashan, had remained

undiagnosed partly because the illness develops slowly over several years with the appearance of subtle signs and symptoms, but mostly because hormone estimations were not available to confirm clinical impressions. They were a striking reminder of the similarity of human condition across time, geographical zones and ethnicities in countries that were struggling to come to terms with modernity.

# Anatomy of a Lesion

SKIMS, a budding multi-specialty institution in Srinagar, raised on the pattern of the two premier institutions of the country (AIIMS, New Delhi and PGIMR, Chandigarh), was staffed mostly by our ex-students and colleagues. They were young doctors, bubbling with enthusiasm and energy for having assumed positions and responsibilities beyond their experience. Even though some of them were relatively unknown to the patients and the lay community, they were eagerly sought after by virtue of their status in the new-found super-speciality institution.

Dr ARM was a young surgeon heading the department of neurosurgery. Having trained at a reputed neurosurgical centre, and having been directly catapulted to the topmost position, he was trying hard to grapple with the tedious task of building the faculty. He was in demand for every conceivable neurosurgical problem.

Mohammad Aslam, a junior civil engineer, consulted Dr ARM for pain and weakness in his left foot. The surgeon made a clinical diagnosis of acute lumbar disc prolapse. The CT era had just dawned in Kashmir. He ordered a CT of the lumbar spine which showed a central bulging disc between the fourth and fifth lumbar vertebrae. He advised disc surgery, assuming that the prolapsed disc was compressing the left fifth lumbar root, resulting in pain and weakness of the foot.

In the close society of Srinagar, where everyone seems to know everyone else, and word of mouth carries great weight, patients often seek second opinions from established names in the profession, especially if surgery has been recommended. It takes physicians an average of five to seven years to build a practice, but it takes surgeons much longer to create a favourable reputation before patients repose full faith in, and choose to get operated by, them.

Mohammad Aslam sought a second opinion from me. He wanted answers to three queries: Did he suffer from a disc prolapse? If so, was surgery the definitive treatment for him? If surgery was necessary, was Dr ARM competent to perform it?

It is the guiding principle in my practice to begin from the beginning with every patient, namely the history and course of the illness. Fortunately, Mohammad Aslam narrated the progression of his ailment like a good story-teller. He mainly complained of intermittent lightning pains in his left foot, occurring over a period of nine months. He described them as flashes and jabs that disappeared as fast as they came, making him wonder if he was imagining the pain. The pain was confined to the left foot, only sometimes did it involve the lower leg, and rarely the right foot as well. It appeared several times during the day, while resting or working. Occasionally, it woke him up at night. Coughing, sneezing, straining, turning or twisting made no difference. There was no history of back pain. He did not remember having lifted a heavy object or having strained his back. In the beginning he ignored the symptoms because of their fleeting nature. But for about a month now, his left foot felt weak and tired while walking. There were no involuntary movements of the limbs, no convulsions, no headaches, no visual impairment or gait disorder.

Mohammad Aslam was a well-built, sturdy young man of thirty. The neurological signs were mostly confined to the left foot. There was a minimal weakness in the left foot muscles. All modalities of sensation were intact. However, when the two feet were touched simultaneously with cotton-wool, the left side ignored the stimuli while the right perceived them. The left plantar reflex was extensor — the big toe moved upward on stroking the lateral border of the foot. The spine was normal in all respects.

To summarise there were three distinct features in the patient all pointing to a lesion in the brain and not in the spine. The pain which the patient complained of did not have the characteristics of root pain. It was suggestive of sensory seizures (epilepsy), which pointed to a lesion in the brain, the cerebral cortex. The extensor plantar response was an unmistakable evidence of a higher level of lesion and not one in the nerve root. The sensory inattention to touch on the left foot was another irrefutable evidence of a cerebral pathology.

Clinically this was a lesion where the motor and sensory areas of the foot are represented high on the surface of the brain, in the frontal area on the opposite side. The most likely possibility was a slow growing tumour.

"I do not think your problem is because of a disc prolapse, Mr Aslam." I said with some degree of certitude.

"Thank you. Allah is merciful. I was apprehensive about surgery. I feel greatly relieved that I do not need it." He beamed like a child who had been spared punishment.

"On the contrary, *you do need* surgery but not in your spine," I said sombrely.

His smile disappeared, his face fell. "What is my problem if not a disc?"

"I believe you don't have a problem there," I pointed at his back, "but right here," I drew an imaginary circle with my index finger on top of his head, at the crown.

He was taken aback by my histrionics. His eyes widened with fear and his cheeks took on an ashen hue.

Perhaps I had got carried away because I had picked a lesion which had been missed by the neurosurgeon — like a kid in a classroom answering a question correctly when others had blundered. Success in our profession is a fair-weather friend. One day you feel wretched when you miss a diagnosis which someone else picked, the next day you feel on top of the world because you hit on a correct diagnosis that others have missed, because by then a new sign may have appeared, a new clue surfaced.

I hastened to put him at ease, "I am sorry I seem to have alarmed you, but that was not my intention. I do not want you opened up at the wrong site."

"But my problem is in the foot and the CT scan has confirmed a bulging disc in my spine. I don't see how the head comes into the picture?" He steadied himself and eyed me apprehensively.

"We call it a red herring, a misleading clue. The bane of medicine is to rest the diagnosis solely or mainly on the result of an investigation rather than the total clinical picture. Sometimes, when we form a hasty clinical impression, or have not exactly figured things out, we tend to clutch at straws in the form of test results, even if they are equivocal, only to be proved wrong because we have shut our eyes to other possibilities. Your case is a perfect example."

"I am totally confused with what you are trying to say!" He was perplexed, even annoyed, as if I were faulting him for the misdiagnosis.

"I must commend you for providing a good account of your problem, Mr Aslam," I said to restore his confidence. "That led me to the diagnosis. The bulging disc in the CT is a minor finding, but I do not see it causing pressure on your nerve roots to explain your foot symptoms. On the contrary, there is enough evidence from your history and the clinical examination that points to a lesion in the brain."

"Do you mean I have a tumour in my brain?" He was alarmed by the sound of his own words.

"That is what the signs force me to believe, but I feel it is nothing sinister."

He looked stunned.

"It may not be exactly inside the brain, but sitting on top of it — a benign tumour, I hope."

"What name do you give it?"

"Meningioma."

"What does that mean?"

"The tumour arises from the brain's envelopes called the meninges. That is why it is called a meningioma."

"How are you sure it is on top of my brain where you put your finger?"

"Because of your story. You said that your pain is mostly

confined to your left foot, but it also appears on the right sometimes. That is a very helpful clue. It is on top of the brain that both feet are represented. That is why I feel almost sure that you have what we call a parasagittal meningioma, sitting on top and slightly to the right of the big venous channel of the brain called sagittal sinus. I am ordering a CT scan of your head to confirm it."

ꙮꙮ

Accompanied by his father, Mohammad Aslam returned a couple of days later with the scan report. It confirmed a walnut sized tumour with the classical features of a parasagittal meningioma. He had already read the report and quizzed the radiologist.

"What comes next?"

"You should go back to your neurosurgeon."

"You mean Dr ARM?? But he made a misdiagnosis. And he may be mad at me for having sought your opinion."

"On the contrary, *he should know*. Go back to him and take along the CT scan."

"What about the disc? Does that need any treatment; another surgery?"

"It is of no consequence."

"But Dr ARM may feel offended!"

"I don't think so. We all make mistakes sometime or other, and there is hardly any doctor who can claim total immunity from making a wrong diagnosis."

His father spoke for the first time. "Sir, to speak the truth, we won't feel safe in his hands now. Why don't you refer my son to a reputed neurosurgical centre? We have no problem travelling to Delhi."

"Now that we have a premier institution in our city, there is no reason to rush every patient to AIIMS. Dr ARM comes with excellent credentials and he should be able to deal with your problem. Besides, he does not have to dig deep inside the brain."

"Do we trust him, then? Do we go by your opinion?" Aslam's father asked with emphasis. "Look, he is my only son, I have pinned all my hopes on him. I have lots of responsibilities."

"*Inshallah*, everything will be fine."

My invocation clinched the issue.

Nearly two weeks later, when I had all but forgotten about Aslam, his father phoned. He started shouting expletives, threatening me with dire consequences. I was shocked.

"Doctor, you got my son killed! You sent him to a butcher! You knew Dr ARM had blundered; you still pushed us into his abattoir! Yes, the neurosurgical operation theatre in SKIMS is an abattoir — I am told patients go walking to the theatre only to return to the mortuary. You knowingly sent my young son to his death! I am not going to spare Dr ARM, nor let you off the hook."

It felt like a lightning bolt.

"What happened?" I stammered.

"Doctor, I have lost my son, lost him because an incompetent surgeon is playing with innocent lives. I know he must have fake degrees. This is the curse of nepotism and favouritism in our land — the ministers and mandarins installing their sons and sons-in-law to positions of authority, letting them play havoc with innocent lives. Patients are being treated as guinea pigs. My son is dead—do you understand that, Doctor? He is DEAD." His last word was like a thunderclap.

"I am extremely sorry to hear that. When did this happen? Can we meet?" I tried to calm him down.

"I know my son is dead. His body is still inside the theatre as I speak with you now. They are making excuses, telling us they are trying to resuscitate him. But I know the hard truth. I see no use meeting with you; I will see you in court. You are an accomplice in murder! All you doctors are in league. For now, I have to bury my son, and bury the surgeon with him ..." He went on and on, without giving me a chance to speak.

I was perspiring, my hands trembling, my heart racing. I did not know what had transpired. Most likely, it must have been a sagittal sinus injury during the surgery. I dropped the phone.

For quite some days I was not myself even as the caller did not execute his threat, nor was there a subpoena. I lost my peace, not because I was scared of a physical assault or trial, but because a young life had been snuffed out. The tragic experience set me thinking again. Somewhere things were going terribly wrong in our system. Was the government really in a hurry to induct professionals to the top posts for which they were neither sufficiently trained nor experienced?

ᢀᢀᢀ

I was trying to drive the tragic saga out of my mind, when Aslam's father announced himself in my clinic. To my surprise, he was a different person from the one who had threatened me on the phone.

"Doctor Sahib, I am grateful for the keen interest you took in my son. I know you did what you thought was the best for him. It was in his destiny to be cut short in his prime," he philosophised. "I came here to apologise for my outburst on the phone that day."

"I did not mind what you said. I have no words to express how sad I feel for you. I know how grieved you must be losing your son. How did it happen?"

"There was uncontrollable bleeding during the operation. A blood vessel near the tumour had opened up.

They transfused six units of blood, but it was all in vain. My son never woke up."

"I feel awful about this tragedy. Your son should not have died, but if my words help in any way to assuage your pain I might inform you that no surgeon can guarantee cent percent success even in the best medical centres. When doctors don white coats and gloves they transform into different beings. They endeavour to stay focused and do their best, and not let anything come between them and the patient. It is like a communion, like one going to pray with nothing between him and his God. But the mind may waver, the hands falter and, in spite of all the care, unforeseen complications may occur even during simple operations. That is our Achilles' heel..."

"I fully realise it. I have nothing against Dr ARM. It is the system that is at fault. In the process, precious lives are lost, and nobody cares. God had ordained only thirty years of my son's sojourn on earth; how could it be longer than that?"

ജരുജരു

# Stroke at Noon

I started the day early with a long futile wait for water. Every time I went to the backyard to find out if the water was running in the supply line, I was disappointed. The faucet eyed me with little sympathy; I thought I heard it give a dry laugh or two, but it shed not a drop of the fluid we took for granted back home in Kashmir. We were left with just a bucket of water from the previous day. I saved it for drinking, not knowing if and when we would receive the 45-minute supply that was pumped into the pipes at about 5.30 every morning. I washed my face and decided to forgo the shave and bath.

It was a busy morning with the patients — nearly all of them fellow refugees from Kashmir in the throes of their first summer in exile, most of them suffering from febrile illnesses, skin diseases, heat exhaustion, dehydration, anxiety, apathy and depression. Lunch held no attraction, for we kept worrying about water, but the tap remained waterless. We had consumed the water saved from the previous day's ration.

Barely had I lain on my bed for a mid-day nap when the doorbell rang. It was 2.30 pm. In my shorts, my torso bare, I went outside to check. It was burning hot, the temperature in the mid-forties. The birds had gone quiet, the leaves wilted, and the flowers that had dared to bloom in the morning had been withered by the merciless sun.

There were two young men at the door, breathless with anxiety, their faces wet and shiny with sweat. They apologised briefly and requested that I visit a patient—their mother. She had been unconscious since noon.

I had stopped home visits, I told them, and going out in that heat was, in any case, out of the question, even suicidal. They begged me to make an exception in this case. Their mother was in very bad shape; they were new to the town and they did not know where to go. Their lodgings were not far off; it would take only a few minutes by car, they pleaded.

Reluctantly, I slipped into a half-sleeve shirt and trousers and got inside my car which, parked in the open, had turned into an oven. The steering wheel scorched my hands. I ran back inside to get a wet towel to cover it. The melting tar on the road had turned into paste and the road spewed venomous vapour as we drove past closed shops through what had become a ghost town — the denizens having fled from the terror of heat, like rats into their holes.

From my lodgings at New Plots I must have driven hardly a mile to Sarwal, when I was asked to stop near the back door of a one-storey ramshackle structure that led into a dark, dingy room closed from all sides — no windows, no ventilators, just three blank walls staring silently at you, and the creaking metallic door that let in what little light there was inside the room. It must have been a stable or a storage shed that had been rented out to this family. It was unbearably hot and suffocating. The temperature inside the room felt much higher than in the open. Living here seemed perilous. A corner of the room with a few pots and pans, cups and glasses, and a stove and gas cylinder seemed like it served as the kitchen. There was a mound of rolled-up bedding, two small trunks, an ancient-looking wooden box and bric-a-brac in another corner; and what seemed like school textbooks strewn in another. In the middle, on a tattered bedcover spread on the bare cement floor, a human figure lay sprawled, watched over by two women. They quickly moved aside as I approached the patient.

She was a sparsely-built middle-aged woman, lying limp and unconscious, breathing fast, froth drying up at the corners of her mouth and leaving crests on her flushed cheeks. Her pulse was racing, her blood pressure low. She was hot and dry. Her temperature was a whopping hundred and seven degrees Fahrenheit!

Armed with a photograph and other documentary evidence, her son had accompanied the patient to the Office of the Relief Commissioner early that morning. She was required to be there for a personal interview in order to complete her application for registration as a 'migrant'—a euphemistic term coined by the officials as a ploy to hide the harsh reality that the Pandits were, in fact, refugees who had been driven away from their homes. On a previous occasion, the son had failed to convince the officials about her bona-fides in absentia. This time, she was there in person.

A long queue of refugees was already waiting to get registered. The office had not opened yet and it was going to take a long time before her turn came, the son realised. He had left her there and asked her to take the bus home after completing the formalities. There was no waiting room, not much shade either to protect the crowd in the open. The sun was already up in the sky, beating down hard on them. They had covered their heads with handkerchiefs, towels and turbans.

She had waited three hours for her turn. When she had returned at around noon, she was flushed, weak, exhausted, tremulous, and unsteady. By the time she drank a glass of water, she was confused and incoherent. She had lapsed into coma soon after.

This was the first case of heat stroke in my twenty-nine-year experience as a doctor. I would come across an occasional case of heat exhaustion in Kashmir during the summer months, but heat stroke was unknown to me except for what I had learnt from text books. Yet, there was no doubt in this case — an elderly frail woman, out in the summer sun, on an empty stomach and without water, waiting long hours in the open. This was certainly an invitation to disaster.

In fact, disaster had struck. The woman had been in a coma for nearly three hours when I saw her. Her attendants had little idea about the gravity of her condition. They did not know where to turn for help. They tried feeding her spoonfuls of water, but it ran out from the corners of her mouth. They fanned her with notebook covers and hand-fans hoping she would revive soon. They were new to the city, new to such intense heat. They had no idea how to prevent or fight heat exhaustion, not to speak of managing a heat stroke. There was no doctor around. Someone had informed them that I was in town and they had rushed to see me.

There was no time to lose. Every minute of delay would send her closer to death. Taking her to the hospital was no use at this stage. It would waste another couple of hours getting there, checking in, shifting her to the ward and starting the treatment for which there was no special arrangement.

I looked around and saw a bucket of water nearby.

"We need to cold-sponge her at once. Give me a towel or a sheet of cloth," I said, and dashed towards the bucket. But before I could pull it near the patient, one of the ladies, possibly her daughter-in-law, seized hold of it and dragged it back.

"Doctor Sahib, this is all the drinking water we are left with for the whole family. We will die of thirst if we spend it all sponging her." She wore an expression of alarm even as she was apologetic.

I was stunned, but it did not take me long to understand their predicament, for I was suddenly reminded about the drought in my own water pipes and wondered if the Waterworks Department had released the day's quota after I left.

"Can we get some ice from somewhere?" I asked.

"There is a shop outside. I hope it is open," said one of the young men.

"Go get a large block of ice," I told him.

He ran out and returned quickly with a slab of ice. I asked them to break it into small pieces. We stripped off the woman's clothes. I passed on a portion of the ice to each of the attendants and directed them to rub it into her skin. Four of them took charge of her limbs and I took charge of the torso. We rubbed and rubbed. The ice slabs melted fast and evaporated, almost vanishing on the burning body of the unconscious patient. She remained dry and hot as before even as another ice block was brought in.

I could not see a fan anywhere. Flies buzzed around the patient in a weird dance, sticking at times on my face and arms; cockroaches darted from different directions; an odd mosquito stung my bare arms. The air was rife with the fumes and fulminations of man and beast.

"Can we move her to a cooler room, a room with some ventilation?" I asked.

"We arrived in Jammu only a couple of months back. We have scoured the whole city. Every nook and corner has been rented out. This is the best accommodation we could find after a long search — just one room for the whole family," said the second young man.

"Can you arrange a fan?"

"I will try and see if the landlord has one that we could borrow," he replied as he ran out of the room, soon to return with the landlord who seemed visibly annoyed at having been disturbed at this unearthly hour when the sun beat people unconscious. He wondered why his tenants were making such a big fuss just because a lady had passed out.

"They are not making a fuss, sir. Can't you see this lady is dying? If you have a spare fan, kindly loan it to them. We will feel very grateful," I said rather tersely.

He scowled and slinked away. Soon he returned with a table fan. It was an old rickety contraption that blew more noise than air. I discarded it soon after — it was just getting in the way.

The rubbing went on for an hour, but the temperature refused to come down. Her body was like a stove that continues to radiate heat even after the fuel has burnt itself out. She remained in deep coma.

I ordered a stomach tube and introduced it through her nostril down the food pipe to feed her chilled water in the hope that it would provide internal cooling and hydrate her at the same time. I passed on this function to one of the young men and departed, asking them to report her status to me after two hours.

By then it was five in the afternoon. The streets were showing signs of life, shops were opening for the evening shift, and there was some vehicular movement. It was hotter than before and my head was swimming. I reached my lodgings, parked the car, and walked straight to the backyard to take a look at the faucet. My heart missed a beat! The water was gushing out — we had left the tap open in the morning. After the struggle for water that I had just had with the patient's family, the sight of water getting wasted was heartbreaking.

I rushed inside to wake my wife up. She was napping after having tired herself out waiting the whole morning and afternoon for the water. We gathered pots, pans and buckets and started filling them with water. We were tenants on the ground floor. My landlord upstairs was also stirred into wakefulness by the cling and clang of the buckets and utensils. He wondered why I had not informed him at once to collect his quota of water rather than having it all to myself. His family trooped down with pitchers and buckets and started filling them, pushing us to the rear while we strove hard to get some more. A battle of sorts ensued for water. And soon, the tap started gurgling and spluttering, whooshing and whistling, and finally, after about half an hour, it ran dry.

It was five-thirty. I sank into my bed, feeling wretched and shaken to the core. I was overcome by a strange revulsion — revulsion for existence itself. This was just the beginning of our first summer. Was this going to be our fate — being driven from our homes to live a beastly existence? Were we destined to die unheard and unsung in exile — dehydrated by the wind, burnt by the sun?

But there was to be no respite, no time to brood and cry, for soon after patients started pouring in at my evening clinic. They informed me that there had been gross voltage fluctuations in the power supply due to excessive demand. The pumps at the waterworks department had broken down that morning as a result of a voltage surge. We would face similar breakdowns in the following months and years.

At seven, the heat stroke victim's son reported that her temperature had come down to a hundred and three degrees, but she was still unconscious. They were pushing chilled water and fruit juices through the tube into her stomach. At nine, when he returned to report her status, I was still examining patients. The temperature had come down to a hundred and two, but she continued to be in deep coma. I asked them to continue sponging her to maintain the temperature below a hundred and one degrees, and to report back in the morning. I realised that the probability of her surviving was remote, yet I kept hoping.

Nobody turned up. I had not even asked her name. Nor had I asked her sons about their hometown in Kashmir. Would she die nameless, unknown and unheard?

But there was a picture of the woman in the obituary columns of *The Daily Excelsior*. She was Ambravati from Gautam Naag in Kashmir, a place famous for its cool springs and shady chinars.

*The heat singes and burns*
*The humidity wets and drenches*
*The one slaps and slashes*
*The other drains and chokes.*
*Then you think of the valley*
*And the home you left behind;*

*You long for the cool breezes*
*You dream of the swirling snows*
*The one poisoned with hatred*
*The other cold with terror.*
*Then you ask yourself*
*Is there anything to choose*
*Between there and here*
*Or, for that matter, elsewhere*
*For humans are alike, everywhere.*
*When they choose to be*
*They are black in their hearts*
*And violent in their deeds*
*Be they your adversaries*
*Or those you call your own.*

# The Final Diagnosis

In August 1985 Aunt Kantayani was admitted to my ward for tubercular meningitis. She was diminutive and thin, delicate and fragile, gentle and kind, and almost unchanged from year to year ever since I knew her. Her speech bore the soft, slow, and tremulous drawl of chronic illness. When I was a little child, she had indulged me with delicacies from her pantry. When I grew to be a school boy, her affections too grew and she treated me like her own son. When I graduated in medicine, I took over from our family physician and accepted the role of caring for my kin, especially my aunt.

Kantayani was a special case, a veritable clinical potpourri. 'Once you graduate as a doctor, you will not need many patients to experiment upon — you have your aunt on whom to try your skills in every discipline of medicine,' joked uncle Baigash who doted on his wife. He was right, for Kantayani never ceased to complain — now of weakness, now of body aches, now of pins and needles, now of poor appetite and indigestion, and always of headaches. Yet, as I came to know her over the years, treating her different ailments at different times, I wondered how much of the symptoms were from organic afflictions, and how much an expression of the challenges of living in a large joint family. Notwithstanding, she was a picture of eternal unwellness and I never tired of examining her when she sought my advice, for Kantayani had handed herself over to me completely and never sought any other doctor all her life. She always prefixed her address to me with *balaie lagaye* (may my years be added to yours), and looked upon me as her saviour. I would hate to betray her faith in me.

Our joint family split up in 1963. I moved with my parents from Rajveri Kadal to uptown Barbarshah. However, our bonds with the ancestral house did not cease – in fact they grew even stronger – nor did the dependence of my relatives on me for all their health concerns slacken. I treated all their medical problems and, after I married Leela, she took care of their obstetric and gynaecological complaints.

This time, Kantayani had come to me with headache and low-grade fever. When I examined her I found her neck stiff. That was an alarm signal and I put her in the ward, performed a spinal tap, examined the cerebrospinal fluid and confirmed the diagnosis of tubercular meningitis.

I had put her in a special room. During the visiting hours, the room would be crowded with visitors. One day, I found her son, Satish, sitting by her bedside. I had not seen him for a long time.

"Hi young man, where have you been? Courting your fiancée?" I remarked as I went near and, in an affectionate gesture, placed my hand casually on the nape of his neck to fondle his long mane flowing down to his shoulders. There, hidden under the bushy hair, was a globular swelling.

"What is this? I feel something here!" I exclaimed. "How long has it been there?"

Satish was around twenty-five, gentle and soft spoken like his mother, short but handsome. He was engaged to a very pretty girl. The wedding was scheduled in six weeks.

He looked at me, surprised. "I am not aware of anything."

"What! Are you telling me that you don't feel this buffalo hump on your neck everyday when you take a shower or brush your hair?"

"Not really."

By now he was quite perplexed. I decided to examine him carefully to make sure it was not the thick nape of his neck that I was mistaking for a lump. He had put on weight, and grown his hair long since I had seen him last.

Satish subjected himself to my examining fingers while Kantayani watched from her hospital bed with trepidation. He was her second son and his wedding was her last parental responsibility. She was keenly looking forward to the celebrations. Was I throwing a spanner in her plans?

There was no doubt about the lump. It was well circumscribed, situated at the junction of the head and neck, almost the size of a small plum, hidden securely under his thick hair. It was superficial, just under the skin but went deep into the neck. It was non-tender, smooth, soft and fleshy. Clinically, it felt like a lipoma, a tumour of fatty tissue. The characteristics of the swelling, coupled with the fact that it was asymptomatic and had grown slowly to that size without his being aware of its existence, indicated that it was, in all probability, a benign growth.

"Is it serious?" Kantayani asked when I looked at her.

"Come on, don't you fret dear aunt. It is just one of those benign lumps." I made light of what was threatening to turn into a tense situation.

"Please tell me the truth; what did you find? May god take me, but spare my son. You know that his life is linked with someone else. I am not worried about myself any more; I have lived my life. Please take care of your little brother. Do you think we should postpone the wedding?" After a long time, she suddenly seemed to have gained the strength to speak so many sentences. Satish maintained a stoic silence.

"I don't think it is of much importance. We could leave it alone for the time being since it does not bother him. Besides, it is out of sight and hidden under the hair. We will keep an eye on it and not let it come in the way of the wedding." I tried to sound breezy, not wanting to add to the mental anguish of this affectionate lady holding her own against a serious infection of the meninges (the envelopes of the brain and spinal cord).

That settled the matter. She did not ask another question, nor did Satish.

Kantayani improved fast and I discharged her from the hospital to continue with the medication at home. By the time of Satish's wedding in October, she was up and about, and in full command. I had always wondered at the storehouse of energy in that petite frame. Everyone spoke of her as having a weak constitution, yet she worked indefatigably and never complained of weakness or fatigue when it concerned her children. She would do anything for them; even give her life if it came to that. During the wedding, she flitted about doing her chores here, there and everywhere, looking after the comfort of the guests, and lavishing her affection on her son and his bride. As a habit, she ate little. It is amazing how little food one needs to stay alive and kicking, yet we never tire of gorging ourselves.

After the wedding ceremonies and functions that lasted a full week, we sat together one day partaking of the first tea made by the bride — a ritual that introduces a new bride to the inner circle of relatives.

When I took leave of the family, Kantayani came to see me off at the door. "Please don't hide the truth; is my son in any danger? I hope no disaster strikes us. Now this girl's future is irrevocably linked to his. Please God, have mercy on my children." Her voice was timorous and tense.

It seemed the lump had not grown, yet we had to go by the golden axiom in medicine: In order to find out the exact nature of any lump in the body it must be excised and subject to a histopathological examination. Fingers can deceive, but not the microscope.

"Please don't worry. We will get rid of the swelling in due course. For now, let us give the young couple time to get to know each other and let the bride adjust to your household. I hope, along with her good looks, she has brought good luck as well."

"*Tathasto*—so be it," she exclaimed and gave me an approving look.

A couple of weeks later, I called Satish to the hospital and took him to my surgeon friend, Dr Bal Krishen Jalali. He agreed with my preliminary diagnosis of lipoma and addressed Satish affably, "Any time of your choosing, young man, and we will yank it off your neck."

"He is just married," I informed him.

"In that case, we could wait. There is no hurry."

Dr Jalali looked at the calendar. "December 25 is my operation day. Will that be Okay?"

"Done," I exclaimed, "there can't be a better day than Christmas."

ꙮ

On Christmas morning, after we moved him to the operation theatre, I wished Satish good luck, and walked to my ward to examine my patients. Barely halfway through the rounds, I was informed that Dr Jalali wanted me in the theatre. I thought he had finished operating and desired me to have a look at the excised growth before he sent it for histopathology.

There was a crowd of relatives in the corridor outside the theatre, looking glum.

"It seems there is a complication..." cousin Inderji said nervously as he saw me.

I dashed inside.

Dr Jalali looked up from the operation table and addressed me in his characteristically easygoing manner, "Well, Kundan, this was totally unexpected. What we have here is a fleshy vascular tumour that bleeds like hell, certainly not a lipoma. I attempted to dissect the area to delineate its extent, but it extends deep and may have burrowed its way inside the spinal canal. I fear it will not be possible to remove all of it. For now, I have taken a large chunk for histopathology."

I looked at the red fleshy mass in the tray. I was certainly not prepared for this. Had we been rather casual with this young man? We had not even taken a routine chest x-ray! Suppose it turned out to be a malignant sarcoma with metastasis to the lungs — we could have avoided surgery in that situation. How would I face my cousin? How would I look the new bride in the eye? How would I explain this to Kantayani? These and more questions assailed my conscience. It was as if a serpent were sitting on the neck of my cousin. The lesson was never to leave a lump, even the most benign looking, alone; never to take any surgery lightly; never to take anything for granted…

Dismayed, I asked Dr Jalali, "What now? Is he stable? Does he need blood?"

"I don't think so; the bleeding has stopped. This certainly is a very unusual tumour. We can plan the next step only after we get the histopathology report. For now, I am going to stitch back the incision."

"I hope it is not malignant," I said and left the theatre, deeply perturbed and guilt-ridden. I was mobbed by the crowd waiting outside, eager to know the details.

"He is going to be fine; we will soon shift him back to the ward," I cut short the queries and offered no details, no explanations. I had yet to come to terms with the findings.

Since it was Christmas, I had planned to finish my rounds early, take a look at Satish and go home to join Usha, my sister who was visiting from the USA. She was waiting to know how the surgery had gone.

ꙮ

New Year eve dawned bright after a cold, frosty week. Dr Abdul Rashid Khan, the pathologist, came to see me in my room.

"I believe Satish is your cousin?" he caught me off-guard. He was armed with the histopathological report on the tumour. "I am sorry the news is not good."

Dr Khan had been one of my brighter students. Tall, lean and balding like me, he would often come to see me in my chamber to share his exploits with the microscope. Of late, he was enthusiastic about a new technique called fine needle aspiration cytology (FNAC). He was perfecting his skills, gaining in confidence every day.

He placed the report on my table. It was a detailed report with the final impression: liposarcoma with islands of tumour mass resembling haemangiopericytoma.

It was a confusing, discomfiting report. It suggested two types of tumour in the same specimen, which was very unusual. While liposarcoma rang alarm bells, I had not heard of haemangiopericytoma.

"It seems you are not exactly sure of what you have seen and reported?" I could take liberties with my ex-student.

"I have seen such a thing for the first time in my experience. I consulted the books, and while I am sure about the liposarcoma, some slides suggest the possibility of haemangiopericytoma," he explained.

"What is haemangiopericytoma?" I asked.

"The books say it is a malignant condition."

"The tumour was quite vascular and bled easily during the surgery," I informed him.

"That confirms my impression. If you desire, you could get a second opinion from AIIMS?"

"My sister, Dr Usha, is in town. She is flying back tomorrow. I might hand over a couple of the slides to her to seek a second opinion from Buffalo."

He rose with a smile of satisfaction at having put his finger on the diagnosis, and started walking off with the familiar tilt of his neck and the drop of his right shoulder. How often do we pat ourselves for having correctly diagnosed a serious pathology, forgetting for a moment that it could be the harbinger of catastrophe for the patient and his family!

Taking the slides from him, I drove home with a heavy heart and a burdened conscience. I had delayed exploration by four months from the time I detected the tumour, and now I had the unenviable task of breaking the grim news to my family and deciding on the next step.

It seemed quite inauspicious to break the tragic news to the family on the New Year; I had to handle the situation tactfully, dropping hints and not revealing just how grim the situation really was. They were dazed when I suggested Tata Cancer Institute. Kantayani gave a loud wail and swooned. Uncle Baigash was stunned, but we were not going to lose any more time. We decided that Satish would leave for Bombay on 7 January along with his brother and brother-in-law.

The send-off to the threesome was sad and sentimental. It was a strange and tragic sequence of events — an affectionate pat on the neck, a chance discovery of a lump, a four-month delay, an unsuspecting surgeon, a pathologist as a harbinger of doom, a newly-married couple under a cloud, a fragile mother in tears, and a family physician with a pricked conscience. Was I seeing off a condemned young man or would God's mercy and benevolence prove the forecast of doom wrong?

ꙮ

Divine mercy has astonishing ways of shining upon its beneficiaries. In our case, it was quickly on its way. When Usha called from Buffalo, it sounded like a voice from the heavens—the sweetest words that we had heard in a long time. "Congratulations! The pathologists here feel it is not a malignant tumour. They have labelled it 'nodular fascitis', a relatively benign condition. It may be confused with a sarcoma, because of which it is also called pseudo-sarcoma. They suggest a total excision of the tumour."

We cried with emotion, hugged each other and danced with joy. Satish and his two companions were already in Delhi on their way to catch the train to Bombay. We rushed to break the happy tidings to his parents, phoned Satish to cancel the journey to Bombay and, instead, report at AIIMS to get the tumour excised.

The gloom lifted and there was jubilation. Aunt Kantayani got up from her bed gingerly and held my hand in her tiny hands, looked into my eyes with infinite gratitude and smiled as I have never seen her smile. She had come to life again. '*Balaie lagaye*' she cooed.

The next day I called Dr Khan to my room and asked him if there could be a mistake in his interpretation of the slides. "We have received the report from Buffalo. They say it is nodular fascitis. I have not heard of it before, but I am told it is a benign condition."

"Where is your cousin now? How is he?" Dr Khan asked.

"He is in Delhi to consult a surgeon at AIIMS. I hope they are able to excise the tumour in its entirety. Of course, we will get another opinion from them after the surgery."

"I will cut some thin sections from another block that is with me, make new slides, and come back to you," he said.

He returned in two days. "I have reviewed the old slides,

and examined the new ones. I agree with the pathologist from Buffalo. There are features of nodular fascitis in one of the slides. But I am not sure about the total picture. There is definite evidence of haemnagiopericytoma in some of the slides." He retained a tone of self-assurance.

Three possible diagnoses were now in contention: nodular fascitis, liposarcoma, and haemnagiopericytoma. What was my cousin suffering from? What was the real, the final *diagnosis*? It seemed now that even the microscope could deceive not just the physician's fingers.

ꕤꕤ

Satish returned from Delhi after three weeks. The next day, he came to our home along with Inderji. I went over the details in the discharge summary from AIIMS. The tumour had been excised. The surgeon had not been able to remove the entire tumour mass; a small remnant that had burrowed inside the vertebrae had to be left behind. The pathologist at AIIMS had reviewed the slides that Dr Khan had loaned, and examined new slides made from the tumour excised at AIIMS.

His *final diagnosis*: High grade malignant haemnagiopericytoma, a highly malignant condition.

The surgeon had given a hopeless prognosis. He was not sure about the future course of action, but recommended radiotherapy all the same, and referred him back to Kashmir to attend the oncology department at SKIMS.

It was a thunderbolt after the temporary reprieve we got from Buffalo.

Inderji asked me if they should start radiotherapy and whom they should contact at SKIMS. Satish showed no emotion. He looked placid as ever, and quiet. He did not ask any questions. I do not think he understood the gravity of the situation. If he did, he behaved like a yogi — impassive and calm in a storm.

It was Sunday. Our family was together at the breakfast table. I looked at the two brothers and their whole childhood flashed back in a kaleidoscopic panorama. They always seemed vulnerable because of their short stature and 'weak' constitution, a feeling magnified by the indulgence and the loving ministrations of their doting mother who would worry herself to death over them. Was Satish finally condemned to a terrible end so soon? Was the report of nodular fascitis from Buffalo just a brief happy interlude in an otherwise tragic scenario? Was it just a cruel joke?

What was the final diagnosis in this young man?

All eyes were on me. There was an uncomfortable silence as I sat there, fiddling with the discharge summary from AIIMS, my thoughts travelling back right to that fateful day when I had patted my cousin affectionately on the nape of his neck. If it was such a terribly malignant condition as Dr Khan had pronounced, and the pathologist at AIIMS had fully concurred with; if there was no established role for any other treatment modality in such a situation, why should we subject Satish to unnecessary interventions? My intuition told me to advise him against radiotherapy.

"I do not think there is any need to rush into radiotherapy. I will speak again with Usha. I will phone the pathologist at AIIMS, and speak with Dr Khan again. Meanwhile, my brother here deserves some time to himself, to recover and recuperate fully from the surgery."

Everyone looked at me in astonishment at this declaration.

The next day, I called Dr Khan over to my chamber. On hearing of the histopathological diagnosis from AIIMS, he jumped with excitement. "I am glad the surgeons and the pathologist at Delhi agree with my diagnosis. I was confident about it; I could face any number of pathologists on this case." Hubris was evident in his demeanour.

I had no reason to fault him. After all he had the backing of pathologists from the premier institution of the country. I admired his self-confidence.

"So you stick to your original opinion and not the revised one you made after I communicated the diagnosis from USA."

"I have every reason to," he grinned; "there were only a few areas that could be confused with nodular fascitis, but the diagnosis of haemangiopericytoma is certain. This is an open and shut case."

I hoped he was proved wrong, even as I did not lose my faith in him as a competent pathologist.

ꕤ

That was 1986. Four years later, there was a mass exodus of Pandits from Kashmir. Kantayani and her family moved to Gurgaon. I settled in Jammu and we hardly ever saw each other. Many of my relatives and friends settled in different towns and moaned that they were deprived of my medical advice on which they had depended all their life.

Aunt Kantayani — petite creature of nature, immutable and unchanging — carried on from year to year in exile. I saw her in 2006 when she came to Jammu to spend time with her daughter, Phoola. She had become even more frail, anaemic and weak. She could barely utter those affectionate words, '*balaie lagaye*'. I ordered tests and confirmed my suspicion of end-stage kidney disease. She returned to Gurgaon to be with her family, where she passed away peacefully after having battled bravely, going through haemodialysis for two years.

One of the pall bearers who lent their shoulders to carry her to the crematorium was her darling son Satish. After the cremation, I walked towards him and put my hand on his neck by the same sudden impulse I had followed in 1985. Twenty three years after that fateful day, there was no evidence of any lump whatsoever.

ꕤ

# A Bizarre Nocturnal Occurrence

Dr. NAM had been my student in Srinagar Medical College. During his student days I treated him for Ankylosing Spondylitis. The condition had started when he was sixteen, and progressed rather rapidly to involve his spine. He could hardly bend his back or move his neck; he had to turn his whole body to look sideways or behind him. Soon after graduation he was posted as a medical resident in my unit. Though he had been an average student, I liked him for his liberal outlook on religion and politics in the highly-charged atmosphere of Kashmir.

During his residency Dr. NAM married nurse Razia. She suffered from diabetes. Together they built a small practice in Anantnag, a town 50 Km south of Srinagar. Within a few years they had set up a nursing home. That was in the 80s. It did not take long for their practice to flourish, and all they desired was to take it to greater heights and stay healthy.

The couple would come down to Srinagar to consult me for their health problems. Razia's diabetes was well-controlled on a twice-daily insulin regimen, and Dr. NAM's joint inflammation remained quiescent for many years, fixing his neck into a permanent leftward tilt. Whenever they came to see me, they bubbled with contentment, thanking Allah for his mercies.

ꕥ

My exodus from the valley in the wake of militancy and violence in 1990 put an abrupt end to my 24-year career in the Medical College and a private practice that I had built assiduously over the years. There was no other way except to move on in life, strike new roots, and establish new relationships. I came to Jammu and settled down to a routine entirely different from the one at home. In the early days of displacement, I missed my students and teaching rounds, and remembered my patients back home in Kashmir, some of whom had been like family members. While most of them had no choice but to consult other doctors, some did seek me out in Jammu. The doctor-patient relationship is one based on trust; a trust that becomes a habit over the course of years, a habit hard to break. It is not always easy for a patient to adjust to a new doctor. You stick to your own doctor just as you stick to your lawyer or barber, milkman or grocer, tobacconist or baker, even though you sometimes feel that you don't always get the best service.

The NAM-Razia doctor-nurse couple receded into some deep recess of my memory, and I hardly thought about them in the travails of exile until the day they landed in my Jammu clinic. We were meeting after seventeen years! They had flown down to consult me for Razia's bizarre recurring nocturnal episodes.

She would wake up all of a sudden in the middle of the night, confused and disorientated. She would sit up and look around as if she were in a strange place. She would fling her arms around, stand up and walk aimlessly around the room, sometimes looking into cupboards, unaware of her husband. In apparent frustration, she would sit down and start thrashing her legs hard, hard enough to hurt herself.

During the first episode Dr. NAM woke up because of the disturbance. He called out to her but she did not respond. He got out of bed, held her arm, and shook her gently to gain her attention, but she looked at him as if at a stranger. He was stunned, wondering if an evil spirit had seized his wife. She resisted when he tried to stop her from beating her legs on the floor. He got her a glass of juice which she refused to drink. After a lot of persuasion, he managed to lead her back to the bed. She went to sleep in a few minutes only to wake up in the morning with no memory of the event. Dr.

NAM had her blood sugar checked. It was 120 mg. He had no explanation for the nocturnal event.

The second episode, nearly a week later, was brief. Razia woke up and went to the bathroom. She closed the door with a bang that awakened her husband. He followed her into the bathroom to find her confused and trying unsuccessfully to untie the string of her pyjamas. He made her sit on the toilet. She came out, sat on the floor, and started thrashing her legs. When he tried to stop her, she looked at him wide-eyed and angry. After a while, she stopped and looked around as if trying to recall where she was. The whole episode was over in fifteen minutes. The next morning she had no recollection of the event.

During the third episode on the following night, she once again woke up confused, got out of bed, moved around aimlessly for a while, sat down and started thrashing her legs on the floor. Her husband rushed to the refrigerator to get her a glass of juice which she spurned with a shove of her arm. The glass fell down and broke, spilling the juice onto her nightdress. It startled her. She looked at him strangely, stood up and walked back to the bed, where she slumped like a rag doll.

Dr. NAM decided to fly to Delhi. He would not trust his wife with anyone in Kashmir for he believed militancy had drained Kashmiris of all values and dehumanised civil society, the medical profession being no exception. He had another reason for travelling to Delhi: the militants had singled out the doctor-nurse couple, allegedly for performing operations like pregnancy terminations and sterilisations, which went against the teachings of puritanical Islam. They had forced a ban on their nursing home during the worst years of the militancy. That was the time he had taken his only daughter away from the stifling atmosphere in which girls were ordered to stay home, wear a hijab, perform domestic chores and memorise the *Quran* rather than going to school and receiving formal education. He would not let his only daughter be shrouded in a veil, confined within the four walls of a house, and in mortal fear of reprisals for defying the diktats of the militants. He had sought admission for her in a Delhi boarding school. She had done well and secured admission into a medical college and was in her third year now. It was time to pay her a visit and, with her help, arrange for a medical examination for Razia.

Several specialists, including a cardiologist and a neuro-psychiatrist examined her. A full biochemical profile was conducted as also a 24-hour holter-monitoring, EEG, MRI of the head, and sleep studies. Various possibilities were discussed including the hysterical conversion reaction and various sleep disorders like confusional arousal, sleep walking and nocturnal frontal lobe epilepsy, etc. The psychiatrist had a few sessions with her and believed she had not taken the forcible closure of her nursing home well. She was under stress and suffering from depression and anxiety that warranted regular medication including a bedtime anti-anxiety pill.

Several weeks passed without an episode. The couple forgot about it like a bad dream. Then it happened again. She woke up confused in the middle of night, moved out of the bed, sat down and started thrashing her legs. After a while she lay down exhausted and sweating and went to sleep on the bare floor.

Dr. NAM flew her Jammu the next morning. Meanwhile, word had spread in Anantnag that Razia was possessed. Others said she was reaping the harvest of her sins.

I found Razia quite cheerful. Seventeen years had not changed her much; she still looked younger than her years whereas her husband had greyed quite a bit and was hunched from the joint affliction. I could not get more out of her story except that she sweated a lot each time she went back to bed after the episodes, which her husband ascribed to the exertion she went through from flinging her arms about and thrashing her legs.

These episodes, she explained, were the result of an evil eye. Militancy had abated to a large extent and the couple had resumed their practice — albeit with a low profile — but people still eyed them with suspicion because of the false stories the militants had spread about the goings-on in their nursing home. Fellow doctors had generally been jealous of their success. It was not unusual for adversaries to seek the help of *pirs* to cast magic spells. Dr. NAM concurred with his wife's explanation of her nocturnal attacks!

Razia was slightly plump, puffy in the face, with mild ankle oedema. She had grade one hypertension. A slight diminution of the sense of touch and vibration in her toes pointed to diabetic peripheral neuropathy. Her urine showed mild protein. Her creatinine was marginally elevated. It was obvious that long-standing diabetes had caused significant damage to the kidneys and peripheral nerves. She kept a tight control on her blood sugar as was evident from the serial blood sugar readings and HbA1c levels that she maintained in a diary.

"I feel your nocturnal occurrences are the result of hypoglycaemia, Razia," I explained.

"I have not recorded her blood sugar during the attacks, but her fasting sugar following the attacks has generally been in the normal range or slightly above normal," Dr. NAM argued.

"That does not discount the possibility of midnight hypoglycaemia. Have you not heard of Somogyi Effect?"

"I have no idea what that means."

"It is a rebound high blood sugar detected in the mornings in response to a big drop in the level during the night in patients on insulin. The rebound is from the compensatory mechanisms that come into play. The danger is that one may end up increasing the evening dose of insulin on finding high morning levels when, in fact, you should be decreasing it. That will certainly lead to more hypoglycaemic episodes during the night."

"That is exactly what I did!" exclaimed Dr. NAM. "I jacked her dose up by two units after her second episode. The third attack followed the very next day. But in none of these bizarre episodes did I find any of the usual signs of hypoglycaemia..."

"Like what?" I asked. I was again being his teacher after all these years and he was the obedient student he had always been.

"I mean fast pulse, sweating, weakness, hunger etc. Nor did she have tremors, convulsions or coma. Do you still think her abnormal behaviour and the thrashing of legs was due to hypoglycaemia?"

"I have no doubt it was hypoglycaemia and nothing else. It is not unusual for patients to behave strangely, as if they are drunk or demented, during an episode of hypoglycaemia. There are reports of patients having been arrested because of the confusion, unsteady gait, disorientation and abnormal behaviour. That the classical signs of hypoglycaemia were missing in the case of your wife could possibly be due to diabetes-related impairment of the autonomic nervous system due to which these other symptoms you just spoke of were masked. Another reason to suspect hypoglycaemia is the presence of kidney damage that may give rise to decreasing insulin requirements. I see that Razia has not changed her insulin dose for several years. The presence of protein in her urine and the borderline abnormality in her renal function tests indicate the onset of kidney damage. It will be worthwhile to monitor her blood sugar levels frequently for a few days, and at least once during the night at about the time she had the episodes. That might give us a fair idea of what is going on."

The couple reported again on the fourth morning. The night blood sugar readings on three consecutive nights between 2 and 3 am had been 78, 87 and 61 respectively — all in the low range. However, there had been no overt symptoms of hypoglycaemia. The daytime readings had remained more or less normal.

The persistently low levels during the nights were highly suggestive. The patient was certainly going into borderline hypoglycaemia almost every night at the present insulin dosage. I advised them to cut down the evening dose by three units and repeat midnight sugar levels.

That dosage worked. The night blood sugar rose to normal levels all through the week. The future dosage was fixed at this level.

"Before we return to Kashmir, I have to ask you one

question that has baffled me all through — why did Razia thrash her legs during the episodes?" Dr. NAM asked.

"It is not totally puzzling. It is well known that the human mind may behave in a stereotyped fashion under physical, biochemical or emotional stress. Such stereotyped behaviour can manifest, among other things, in the form of a persistent mechanical repetition of speech or movement. In the case of your wife, it was the low blood sugar that triggered the bizarre behaviour. You already know that the brain depends entirely on sugar as a fuel for its normal functioning."

He burst into unrestrained laughter, tears streaming down his eyes. "Imagine, I had almost come to believe in hexes and curses!"

# Tenderer than a Petal, Harder than Stone

I had finished examining Shyam Lal. While he was going out, Shobavati was helped in by her husband. Just as Shyam Lal left the room, his son turned back to ask me, "Doctor Sahib, what are the chances for my father?"

"Chances?" I was not sure what exactly he wanted to know.

"I mean, how long does he go on like this? He seems to make no headway. What is the prognosis?"

His father was a patient of chronic renal failure from long-standing diabetes and hypertension. Besides his diabetes being quite brittle and difficult to manage, and his blood pressure resistant to a combination of three antihypertensive drugs, he was prone to repeated urinary tract infections from an enlargement of the prostate, that gave him fever and chills. As a result, his renal status was deteriorating fast.

"His prognosis is not encouraging. His renal function is grossly compromised. As of now, he is carrying on without dialysis, but it will have to begin sooner rather than later. If we make a shunt now, it will come in handy when dialysis becomes necessary."

"Is he in immediate danger? How long do you think my father will survive, with or without dialysis?" he finally asked, without mincing words.

"I can't say with any degree of certitude. Humans are tenderer than petals, and also harder than stone. That is what my mother used to say, and I agree with her after my long experience as a doctor. Healthy-looking people drop dead from a sudden heart attack or brain haemorrhage, while chronic patients linger on from one year to another," I replied.

He seemed rather confused, and left before I could elaborate on his father's condition.

Shobavati had been listening to this dialogue with interest, nodding her head while she waited to be examined. When I turned my attention towards her, she smiled at me appreciatively, her false teeth flashing in her mouth.

"Doctor Sahib, you were explaining the nature of our bodies to the son of the patient who left. What do you think of me? Am I a stone or a petal?" She asked in her slow, staccato speech.

Shobavati, seventy-five, had been my patient for several years. This time she had come for pain in her left arm that made her miserable. She could not raise the arm above the shoulder level. Nights were especially difficult. Turning in bed woke her up with a sharp pain and combing her hair was not possible without help. A case of chronic ulcer dyspepsia, she had been nursing knee pain from osteoarthritis for several years. Eight years earlier she had developed complete heart block for which she had been fitted with a pacemaker. Three years later a revision pacemaker was necessitated when she developed lead infection in the first. She sustained her first stroke a year after; it gave her weakness in her left arm and a speech defect. The arm weakness resolved to a large extent, but some speech disorder persisted, and her left shoulder started aching. She had sustained another stroke the previous year, now on the other side of brain, which left her with partial loss of function in her right hand.

In spite of her multiple problems and handicaps, Shobavati retained her poise and charm. She was very graceful for her age, her eager brown eyes sparkled in her sunken orbs, and the *dejhour* dangled delicately from her ears as she moved her head. She looked the quintessential Kashmiri Pandit matriarch.

"Shobavati, you certainly are a tender petal, pretty

and delicate," I replied. Looking at her husband who was watching with interest, I asked, "Don't you agree, sir?"

He gave an uncertain smile.

"Thank you, Doctor Sahib, you flatter me. I am no tender petal, but I sure am harder than granite. Look how each disease chips a piece off me. Yet I go on living. I diminish, but I refuse to perish."

"You are poetic; and humorous too. Humour adds years to life," I complimented her.

She gave a shy but grateful smile.

"But how long do I have to suffer? When do you think my time will come?"

"Our lifespan is predetermined," I replied. "I tell you this in spite of being a man of science. When the end has to come, a minor illness, like a small whiff of air, may blow a person away. Like the leaf from a tree that has withstood storms but falls to a gentle breeze. Your time will come when it has to."

"I hope it comes soon. I have been putting up with one scourge after another. My nights are restless; my husband has to remain awake when I cry in pain. I went through those heart attacks when I would just pass out for no reason until I was given the pacemaker. I had my kidney removed way back for a huge stone that gave me repeated infections. I did not think of it again. My uterus and ovaries were scooped out of my abdomen when I was still young, yet I survived with dignity. The biliary colic that made me toss with pain is a distant memory after the gall bladder was removed. Two attacks of paralysis did not make me as miserable as the shoulder."

"You really are like a precious stone, a diamond that has been chiselled from time to time to get the best cut that makes you scintillate," I said laughing.

"In the process I am getting lighter every time I lose a chip."

"Yes, you are light like a flower yet hard like a diamond," I continued with the banter.

"Not without purpose. I have discarded my body parts in advance; I believe it has made me lighter for the final journey. The pall bearers will have an easy time carrying me."

I laughed aloud and replied appreciatively, "You really are full of wit, Shobavati."

"I am, but the pain in my arm has plagued my existence. I think it will kill me."

"Come on, it is just a frozen shoulder that never killed anyone."

"But, as you said, it does not need a hurricane for a tender petal to fall down…"

"Everything in its time, dear Shobavati," I said, helping her out of the chair.

# The Mover of Chess Pieces

## I

Sarla Bhan, forty-four, sought my consultation for low mood and loss of sleep.

Distress was writ large on her shiny, round, pink face. Anxiety furrowed her brow and oozed from her bearing and speech.

She was shy of sharing her story. When probed and prodded, she burst into tears. Nurse Kiran offered her a tissue and gave her an affectionate hug while I gently patted her shoulder. That did the trick, and she opened up amid sniffles and sighs. It was a poignant tale.

Along with son Abhishekh, she was forced to move to Jammu in 1990 in the wake of terrorism that had gripped Kashmir valley. It was with great difficulty that she was able to find a room to live in. She could not have lived in a tent like the other refugees, for seven-year-old Abhishekh was afflicted with cerebral palsy that she ascribed partly to a mismanaged delivery, partly to a birth defect, and mainly to her stars. While there was help back home in Kashmir, Sarla found herself alone in Jammu and it was hard to cope with her severely disabled son. Her husband, Chaman Lal, a State Bank employee, had decided to stay back or his job would be terminated, and the family would lose all their source of sustenance.

It took Chaman Lal fifteen months to persuade his employers to transfer him to Jammu. His arrival eased the situation for Sarla, but he was transferred to Kanpur only after a brief stint, from where he could visit his wife and son for a couple of days every month. Meanwhile, Abhishekh was getting heavier and more difficult to manage. He had to be assisted for everything — feeding, washing, grooming, bowel and bladder care. Worse, he was prone to recurrent seizures that defied treatment. Sarla pined for a girl child. That, she believed, would fulfil the twin objectives of having a helpmate and a daughter. But a second child did not arrive, nor did they seek medical advice, afraid that the next child could also be born with the same disability.

The couple was on the lookout for help. Was it divine intervention that a family friend came forward with a unique proposal? He was an engineer in faraway Kishtwar in a Central Government-sponsored hydroelectric project. An orphan lad from Manipur had landed on the site in search of a job in the project. He had two little sisters with him. The engineer was looking to adopt a child and here was the opportunity. He absorbed the lad in his office as a peon, and offered to adopt one of the sisters. The lad readily agreed and requested him to help find another family who might adopt his second sister. The engineer phoned Sarla and Chaman Lal. The couple jumped at the offer. Chaman Lal travelled to Kishtwar and adopted the little girl, Nandu. They named her Nandita.

Nandita was a boon. She quickly adapted to her new home, helped Sarla in domestic chores, bonded with the spastic child and looked after him like an elder sister. Finding her sharp and intelligent, Sarla enjoyed tutoring her.

Chaman Lal was moved around every three or four years by his bank, serving at different stations for different durations, with several postings in and around Jammu as well. Nevertheless, they carried on, and even managed to build a two-storey house on a modest plot of land. That gave them renewed confidence, like the old times when they had their own home in Kashmir.

Sarla could not believe how swiftly time had passed when she celebrated her son's twenty-second birthday. That day, she looked at Nandita – nearly as old as her son – as if for the first time, and realised she had reached marriageable age. Yes, she had grown into a pretty young woman, coy and conscious of herself. Sarla's heart missed a beat. What if she had to part with this girl that she had grown so intensely fond of – her companion and confidante, her daughter and helpmate, and a caring sister to her invalid son?

But every daughter has to marry at some time, bid goodbye to her parents' home and start her own. That, Sarla was convinced, is the *dharma* of every mother, yet the nagging fear that she would lose Nandita and her small world would collapse like a house of cards, dogged all her waking and sleeping hours, and snatched her fragile peace of mind. At the same time, she could not bear the thought of her daughter wasting away as a spinster. Chaman Lal tried to put her fears to rest, but she lost her tranquillity, grew anxious, lost her sleep and came close to a nervous breakdown. That is when she came to consult me.

While I listened to her engaging story, she turned out to be a kind and sensitive person, prone to anxieties, but quite suggestible.

"There is always a way out," I said.

"But I don't see any!" she cried, bursting into tears again.

"You will not send Nandita away; you will bring home a husband for her, a live-in groom," I said. It was not an uncommon practice back home in Kashmir to persuade a prospective groom from a poor household to live with the bride's family.

She jumped at the suggestion. "Oh! Why did we not think of that? Look, how befuddled our minds have become. We will get in touch with the matchmakers right away. Thank you, Doctor Sahib, you have solved my problem! But won't you write some medicine for my sleep?" The transformation was sudden.

She left in a cheerful mood.

Hope smiled, and flowered soon. A few months later, a beaming Sarla came to deliver the invitation card. She had stopped taking the pills I had prescribed. She was busy making arrangements for the wedding. Nandita was going to wed Sanjay, a Jet Airways employee. He was a fatherless child, the younger of two siblings brought up by their mother in great hardship. The older brother was already married and had a child. It did not matter to Sanjay's mother if he lived with his in-laws as long as the family lived in Jammu. Their small home was already cramped — there was hardly any space for an additional member.

II

Nearly a year and a half later, Sarla was back in my consulting chamber, tense and agitated. "I am sorry to bother you once more, but I have lost my bearings again. I can't give attention to my son; I am nervous and fretful; my sleep has disappeared."

"What is bothering you now?" I asked.

She narrated her story:

"The live-in arrangement did not last long. Sanjay and Nandita were barely ten months with us, when they informed me about their desire to move out and be on their own. I was shocked. I begged them to stay on, offered alternatives and incentives, including a separate kitchen under our roof. But they had made up their mind and I realised that it would be wrong to stand in their way. I did not want to lose them forever; I blessed them in their venture, gifting them my best kitchenware, bedding, and other necessities for setting up a new household. This was the least I could do for my daughter who was stepping into a new life."

"You are a brave woman," I said admiringly. She had steeled herself through a life of hardship, looking after her disabled son, living through the vicissitudes of exile and the frequent transfers of her husband.

"But their departure has been a hard blow. I have grown intensely anxious and forgetful, unable to think or concentrate on any task. I have lost my sleep, and the will to live."

She was quite depressed.

"You have shown great fortitude all your life. You have pulled through worse crises — why should you react the way you're doing now? After all, Nandita is still in town. She must be visiting you now and then."

"It is six months since Nandita and Sanjay left," she replied in a dull voice, "they had promised to visit me every week, but she came just four or five times..."

"Doesn't she phone you?"

"Of course, she phones... sometimes, but my heart craves to see her. The last time she came to see me, she looked exhausted. I asked her to come back home to recuperate. I thought she was losing her health because of the stress of living alone in a rented place. But she said she would be fine. However, last week I came to know that they had moved to live with Sanjay's mother and were planning to add another floor to the house. Is that not cheating? In the first instance, she lied to me that she and Sanjay wanted to be on their own. And now, she kept it from me that they had moved back to live with Sanjay's mother."

"She would probably have told you sooner or later," I surmised, trying to make light of her disappointment.

"That is poor consolation, Doctor Sahib."

"But not a false consolation, I can tell you. From what you have told me about Nandita, I feel she is frank and without malice."

"I spoke to her on the phone. I asked her why she had to build when my house was at their disposal — I would gladly transfer the ownership to her. She replied that Sanjay's mother wanted them near, now that she was five weeks *pregnant.* I was stunned that my daughter had also kept her pregnancy from me." Sarla started crying again.

"Come on, you are being too judgmental. You know quite well that your daughter would have shared the good news with you in due course. Don't forget, she was devoted to you all the years she spent under your roof," I reminded her. "The arrival of a baby should give you joy. You will be a grandmother in a few months; you need to celebrate."

"I feel I have been cheated. Maybe I am growing old, insecure, unsure of myself."

"I don't think so; you still look young and healthy. You should be proud of being a crusader all your life. "

The consultation had stretched to half an hour and I did my best to counsel her, explaining the trials each one of us had to face in life, praising her for her sacrifices, her virtues as a mother, her compassion in accepting and treating Nandita as her daughter, her eagerness to arrange her wedding to a decent boy, and finally, her spirit of renunciation in offering her house to an adopted daughter. She was a true *karmayogini*, I declared, and God would reward her for her righteousness. All she had to do was to live life as it came and hope for better days.

"But it seems better days are not for me; God is devising worse ordeals for me every time. Just when I see a ray of hope in my life, he envelops me in darkness again," she despaired.

"He is a master gamesman, a chess player who moves us like pawns at will. But don't lose hope; just watch how

He makes the next move to bring a transformation in your life." I spoke from an unexplained gut feeling.

Sarla looked at me as if I was some sort of a soothsayer. The tense muscles of her face relaxed. "If you say so, it must happen, Doctor Sahib. It happened the last time."

She got up, took the prescription, thanked me, and left.

III

I all but forgot Sarla till she reappeared again after a lapse of nearly six years. She sat in the chair and said, "Doctor Sahib, I am down in the dumps again. Please help me. Tell God to move the pieces favourably for me; He may yet listen to you."

I failed to recognise her and to comprehend what she was talking about. This was an enigmatic petition from a patient.

"You seem to have forgotten me; I am Nandita's mother."

A faint recollection of her story echoed from the depths of my memory, but I could still not recall all of it. She had grown plump, streaks of grey at her temples, fine lines on her forehead and cheeks. Moreover, I was seeing her for the first time with glasses that gave her quite a changed look.

"Oh, it is coming back... You had a relapse from depression when you came to see me last," I said after I looked at her file with my prescriptions neatly stapled. "You never came for a follow up."

"I felt fine; I did not feel the need to report back. Your last words still ring in my ears. I started on the medication you advised and got better every day, reminding myself of your words. You were prophetic. You spoke about God moving us like chessmen. That is what has been happening."

She spoke as if I remembered her whole story by heart. It was after more questioning that I got back on track. And I recalled that her daughter along with her husband had left her to be with his mother.

"Tell me what happened." I was keen to hear more of her story.

"That time, I had lost all hope before I saw you, but I returned home in a positive frame of mind. By a stroke of good fortune, my husband was transferred back to Jammu, this time, fortunately, to a branch of the bank just next to our house. That was the first sign of a turnaround in my luck. It buoyed up my hopes, for God had moved a piece in my favour. My husband's presence in the house made life much easier and I did not miss Nandita's support. However, I kept open my communication channels and phoned her almost every day, inquiring about the state of her health, and the baby that was growing in her womb. She would visit me occasionally, but I never asked her to come back and live with us. I was happy in her happiness. I remembered your words and they kept my faith alive. Then another miracle happened. The great chess player moved another piece!"

I was listening with rapt attention, wondering…

"It was three and a half years after they left home that

my daughter and her husband returned to live with us, now with a child as an additional gift. I had my daughter Nandita back, a second son in Sanjay and a grandson, Anubhav! He is such a lively child! I had no idea what it meant to have a normal healthy child. It was such a treat to play with him."

"I am so glad for you."

"You gave me hope and made it happen!" She looked at me gratefully.

I nodded my head uncertainly, but she reminded me, "The chess pieces, remember?"

"Oh well, yes... Why did your daughter come back to you?"

"It was not easy to add another floor to their house. The costs had spiralled, the baby was arriving, and Sanjay's job gave him little time to oversee the construction. After the baby was born, I went to felicitate them. I realised that they were cramped for space with not enough room even for the cradle, but I did not open my mouth. A year later, on his first birthday, it pained me to see that the child had no space to toddle around. He kept bumping into doors and windows. It mad me sad and I could not hold myself back; I renewed my offer to Nandita, taking her mother-in-law into confidence. She said she had no problem if her son and daughter-in-law agreed to move to our place."

"She was being practical," I remarked.

"Exactly! They might have been waiting for the offer.

It must have been hard for the extended family to live in that small house. We made a formal deed bequeathing our ground-floor to Nandita. Of course, the whole house will be theirs when we are gone…"

"Why may you think of going? You are not old; there is still a long way to go. Haven't you already made enough sacrifices?"

"All for my son, Abhishekh. Somehow, I know Nandita will not ditch me. She will take care of him after we are no more."

"I hope you have many fruitful years together. There is no doubt your adopted daughter is genuinely devoted to you."

"Thank you for encouraging me. In fact, something good happened. My husband was promoted to a senior position and retained in Jammu for another year after which he decided to go for voluntary retirement. In the process, he got a good deal. We now have all our time together."

"In that case, I see no reason for the relapse of your anxiety disorder."

"You are right; we could hardly believe the good fortune, basking in family love, living in happy, harmonious ambience. Maybe, our own evil eye struck us… suddenly now my mother has taken seriously ill. She lives with my brother in Bangalore and I have not been able to visit her for several years. I would like to be by her side for some time before anything happens to her, but Nandita is in a family way. She is full-term. Her blood pressure is high so the doctor has directed her to take complete rest. He warned that she might develop complications, suffer convulsions, and even lose the baby. Sanjay's mother is ill and he has moved for some time to look after her. I cannot go to Bangalore and leave my husband alone to take care of everyone — my son, grandson and Nandita. I can't handle the anxiety. I wonder how the chess pieces will move to make it all well again... Show me the way; you are a sage!"

Had Sarla come to seek me as a practitioner of medicine to treat her anxieties or as a godman who would solve all her problems?

"The pieces will move as ordained. You must visit your mother. Give your husband a chance; it is time for him to prove that he can rise to the occasion. I am sure he will manage while you are away. After all, you will not be gone long."

"How do you know I won't be gone long? Is it going to be the end for my mother?"

"It is for the grandmaster to decide whether He wants to remove a piece from the chessboard or not. His ways are inscrutable; we have to accept His moves gracefully."

"You are speaking in riddles."

"I am only encouraging you to go see your mother," I said, resuming a more down-to-earth tone. "Now, don't fret and worry. I will give you pills to calm your nerves. While you are gone, everything will fall in place. Don't forget the mover of chess pieces."

"I will not; thank you for clearing the fog from my mind."

Sarla stood up, took the prescription and left, calmed down to some extent.

IV

Sarla came to see me again after a fortnight. For the first time since I knew her, she entered my chamber with a jaunty step, smiling, her brown eyes lit up in joy.

"I have not come to see you as a patient; I am here to thank you for all you have done for me!" she said, and suddenly she held my hand and kissed it a couple of times.

I looked at her, bemused. It was gratifying to see her elated, almost euphoric.

"It seems everything has turned out well?"

"It happened exactly as you predicted. It was providential; I had thc good fortune to have the last *darshan* of my mother. I could not have timed it better, for she passed away peacefully the day after I reached Bangalore, as if she had been waiting for me. She breathed her last in my lap. I was fortunate to have the opportunity to pour *Ganga jal* in her mouth and to perform all the rituals, including the tenth day ceremony. I have no regrets; I am contented."

"And how is everything at home?"

"Nandita had gone into premature labour. She was shifted immediately to the hospital where she delivered a baby girl. There were none of the complications we had feared. She was home on the next day. The baby is angelic; she was born the day mother left this world. My mother has not died; she has taken birth again, now as my granddaughter! The master chessman took one piece away and planted another in its place! Doctor Sahib, I am so happy."